P Practicable

P_a Professional Architecture

P Practice

Now you could think about how to proceed with creating successful, usable and award-winning project-buildings; realistically; highly admired by the owners, users, and the surrounding community. Further attainments could be instrumental regarding fulfillment of the professional expectations related to economic aspects of the ongoing business practice. This book is presenting how to progress- with such methodologies, strategic management of the design excellence, constructability, and final elements of resulted architecture practice.

Copyright © 2019 by Kalavati Somvanshi, FAIA.

ISBN   978-1-970160-54-3   Ebook
ISBN   978-1-970160-55-0   Paperback

All rights reserved. No part of this publication may be reproduced, distributed, or transmitted in any form or by any means, including photocopying, recording, or other electronic or mechanical methods without the prior written permission of the publisher. For permission requests, solicit the publisher via the address below through mail or email with the subject line "Attention: Publication Permission".

EC Publishing LLC
11100 SW 93rd Court Road, Suite 10-215
Ocala, Florida 34481-5188, USA

Ordering Information:
Quantity sales. Special discounts are available on quantity purchases by corporations, associations, and others. For details, contact the publisher at the address above.

www.ecpublishingllc.com
info@ecpublishingllc.com
+1 (352) 234-6201

Printed in the United States of America

WELCOME &

GOODLUCK!

P Practicable

Pa Professional Architecture

P Practice

Publication: April 2018

for Somvanshi & Parab family

P Practicable

Pa Professional Architecture

P Practice

By

Kalavati Somvanshi, FAIA

This page has been left intentionally blank.

Copyright Holder

Copyright holder: Kalavati Somvanshi, FAIA

No part, procedure, and expression covered by this book should be rewritten or copied in any form, technological instruments or methods by proceeding with graphic, electronic, mechanical, photocopying, recording, taping or using information for producing another book, storage document or in their professional practice document process. It is not acceptable without the written permission of the author and copywriter-holder in writing.

Disclaimer:
All photographs, diagrams, and text used in producing this book have been initiated, created and written by the author and do not present or proceed with similar or any specific actions by other editors and publishers except where noted in the book.

Claimer:
Photographs and diagrams on page nos. 26, 27, 32, 33 and 50 are sent to me and are approved to include in the book by Misra & Associates, Architects, PC, New York, NY. The designed projects and construction working drawings shown on the same pages were outlined, managed and handled by me as a senior associate in the same firm, to create the design and complete the documents of the same projects.

ISBN   978-1-970160-54-3   Ebook
ISBN   978-1-970160-55-0   Paperback

Editor and research: Kalavati Somvanshi, FAIA
Computer graphics: Kalavati Somvanshi, FAIA
Book Layout Design: Kalavati Somvanshi, FAIA
Freehand graphics, diagrams, photographs (except listed above under 'Claimer'), and cover design: Kalavati Somvanshi, FAIA
If the publisher has inadvertently omitted any credits, the publisher will endeavor to incorporate its revision in the future edition.

Contents

Preface   10

Feasibility Study   12   CONTENTS - 13
                                                                 14   PROCESS
                                                                  14   DESIGN ASPECTS
                                                                  15   SITE CONDITIONS
                                                                  15   CODE APPROVALS
                                                                  16   FEASIBILITY STUDY-
                                                                              DETERMINATION
                                                                              BY THE CLIENT

RFP   18   CONTENTS - 19
(Request for proposal)   20   REQUEST FOR PROPOSAL
                                                                       (RFP)
                                                                       FIRMS AVAILABILITY
                                                                       ARCHITECTS' SELCTIONS-
                                                                       OVERALL QUALIFICATIONS
                                                              21   WORKING PROCESS &
                                                                       SPECIALTY
                                                              21   FORTHCOMING WORKING
                                                                       PROJECT
                                                              22   CONSTRUCTION
                                                                       SUPERVISION

Schematic Design   24   CONTENTS - 25
                                                               26   PRECONCEPTION OF THE
                                                                       SCHEMATIC DESIGN
                                                                       PRELIMINARY DESIGN
                                                                27   APPLICATION OF THE
                                                                       PRELIMINARY DESIGN
                                                                28   TO BEGIN THE PRELIMINARY
                                                                      DESIGN - SITE APPROACH
                                                                29   SITE & PROPERTY PLANNING
                                             & 31   PRELIMINARY DESIGN LAYOUT
                                                                       30   SETBACKS, HEIGHT LIMITS, BUILDING
                                                                       FOOTPRINT & DRAINAGE SYSTEMS
                                                                  32   SCHEMATIC DESIGN PROCESS
                                                                  34   CLIENT STRATEGY & FLOOR
                                                                       PLANNING
                                                                  36   ENTRANCE LOBBIES
                                         37 & 38   INTERIOR STAIR & SURROUNDING AREA
                                                                  39   FLOOR PLANNING

                                                                  41   SURROUNDING AREA AND VIEWS
                                42, 43 & 44   FLOOR PLANNING
                                                                  45   FIRE DEPARTMENT ACCESS

Contents

                    46 PROJECT DEVELOPMENT & ORGANIZATION
47 DESIGN AND DOCUMENTATION PROJECT SCHEDULE
48 EXTERIOR DESIGN
50 WORKING MODELS
52 RESIDENTIAL HOUSE PROJECT
53 RESIDENTIAL HOUSE MODEL
54 HIGH-RISE RESIDENTIAL BUILDING
55 BUDGET ESTIMATES

Design Development

56 CONTENTS - 57
58 SCOPE OF WORK: PLANNING ASPECTS
59 SPACE PLANNING
60 EXTERIOR WALL DESIGN AND DETAILS
61 DESIGN DEVELOPMENT SUPPORTED WITH WORKING MODELS
61 BUDGET ORGANIZATION AND BUILDING MATERIAL SELECTIONS
62 CONSTRUCTION PROCESS, INTERIOR DESIGN AND MATERIAL SELECTIONS
63 WINDOWS, CURTAIN WALLS AND DOORS
64 SPECIFICATIONS

Interior Design

66 CONTENTS - 67
68 INTERIOR DESIGN PROCESS EMERGING PRESENTATION OF THE DESIGN FOR THE CLIENTS
70 PAINTING AND COLOR SELECTIONS
72 TWENTY-FIRST CENTURY ADVOCATING INTERIOR DESIGN PROCESS
73 BIDDING PROCESS AND CONTRACTS FOR INTERIOR DESIGN UNITS

Contents

Construction Documents
74 CONTENTS - 75
76 CONSTRUCTION DOCUMENTS
77 MAJOR DOCUMENT SHEETS
78 SITE CONDITIONS
79 FLOOR PLANS
80 ROOF PLANS
 BUILDING SECTION
81 EXTERIOR ELEVATIONS
82 CONSULTANTS' WORK STATUS
83 SPECIFICATIONS
 REALISTIC CONSTRUCTION
 PROCESS VS. STANDARD
 CATEGORY

Bidding Process
84 BIDDING PROCESS & CONTENTS
85 BIDDING PROCESS &
 BIDDING PROCESS SUGGESTIONS

Project Site Supervision
86 CONTENTS - 87
88 PROJECT SITE SUPERVISION
89 SITE ISSUES, RELATIVE ACTIONS &
 FINAL CONSTRUCTION RESULTS

PREFACE

Preface

Kala believes that all great architecture starts with the concept of the building in its unadulterated form and the process of creating the building—from generic ideas through completion—must remain faithful to the design concept as well as adhere to pragmatic building construction restraints and methods.

As a result, the surrounding neighborhood community would support these types of projects, mostly because they gratify to enhance the social, environmental, and economic importance of their cities. Of course, the urban planning and city planning is also a part of such result. Urban Design, as an inter-disciplinary subject utilizes elements of many built environment professions, including a landscape architecture.

Intentionally, these 'best practices' can be implemented numerous times to aid initial design excellence processes, to achieve successful document submissions, and to adhere to planned construction technology. Such operation could acquire many design awards from related sources; AIA, the Design Excellence, Architectural Record, the Merit Award, Interior Magazine and, would be featured in numerous newspapers, magazines, and books.

To effectuate all aspects of the project, we need to handle it with schedules, charts and design excellence, lists of drawing standards and overall planning, ranking many substantial size projects and additionally, advocating with codes and city agencies' approvals for building the projects. Kala's focus on translating the design into built forms included an overall project schedule to pursue design intent, historic preservation, interior and exterior renovation, the development of technical standards, and one-on-one working sessions.

This book presents the above acts and process to gain the success of **Practicable Professional Architecture Practice (PPaP)** for the junior qualified or practicing architects as per their decisions and efforts. They could succeed in their practice along with achieving reasonable fee status. As one would start this process, they could follow, rethink, and acquire the proposed possible efforts demonstrated in the list of 'Book Contents' noted on the pages 7, 8 and 9. As professionals find an individual process in every stage apparently common, but not commonly found in the profession, they will lead toward their prosperous practice.

First, when relevant to new projects or decisions about particular usage and renovation of buildings, **Feasibility Study** apply for going forward. Feasibility studies are conducted before the process of designing and building on the property. It usually involves gaining approvals for various items from concerned agencies, performing necessary tests on the property to determine the quality of the land or to rectify measures to be taken related to future advanced construction.

Besides, before starting the work process on the projects, many clients want to review architects' selection and firms' ability, experience, and staff availability related to the similar type of project. It requires to tackle and submit the **RFP (Request for Proposal)** to gain the approval of starting the project by succeeded firms or a practicing architect.

PREFACE

As a theory of dealing with the **Schematic Design process** of reasonably medium-to-large-sized projects, most of the time it is recommended that architects and designers integrate a preliminary design phase in their design process. Initial design starts with giving shape and form to counsel and include the client's decisions regarding their earlier expectations. It takes into consideration the style of architecture to be formal or not so formal, classical, historical, industrial, educational, cultural, Western or Eastern, European or of a method belonging to other countries.

During the **Design Development** phase, it is necessary to confirm the planning aspects and proceed with finalizing the plan dimensions to include most construction dimensions of the thickness of walls, all mechanical, plumbing, electrical, and media with unit spaces. With such process, the expected program areas are saved and are available as results during completion of the construction documents and contractors' construction process.

Before this technical aspect, it is prudent to start the process during the schematic design stage utilizing the initial intentions of the original design process. Creating-**working-model** guides, suggests and leads the architects toward the **exterior and interior design** because the models present spatial review and shapes, supporting to think further about the visual impact of the exterior and interior spaces and details.

To create and finalize the material selections and design decisions, the designers should start the **Interior Design process**. However, colors and shapes, furniture design and spacing, impact and support the many aspects of the whole design, including the client's acceptance of it. Interior design decisions related to space availability, design status and the visual impact of furniture affects the planning and the construction documents.

Starting with the **Construction Document** phase, the architects should continue with the entire thought process of construction phase while completing the material details and availability because it could affect the material quality, installation timelines, and impact of weather temperature at specific locations during the construction process for the building and the surrounding site improvement.

Also, some indications have been noted to deal with and succeed with final construction result in the construction phases aside from a regular version of the building construction.

During the **Bidding Process**, architects help to provide the set of drawings, specifications, surveys, and some of the code approval aspects and explanations of the relevant project items. Therefore, the clients could adequately arrange to achieve the **Bidding Process** submissions by the contractors.

Finally, the genuine **Site Supervision** is a successful method of finalizing the completion of the award-winning and extraordinary achievement of most of the projects.

Feasibility Study

Feasibility Study

Feasibility studies can be used as the primary focus for a proposal of architectural project agenda. Later on, when the client decides to select and hire a professional architect, it is essential for the architect to proceed with the earlier skills in architecture and the beginning of schematic design by reviewing the previous feasibility study by the same or other architects, engineers or other professionals. After such consideration of the feasibility study documents, the client can decide to consummate beginning the design and complete construction documents of their project at their specific sites.

For example, this is a critical access and status to deal with large projects and to confirm the appropriate location of sites as well as to proceed possibly with an intricate arrangement of a contract.

Feasibility Study

Contents:

PROCESS

DESIGN ASPECTS

SITE CONDITIONS

CODE APPROVALS

FEASIBILITY STUDY-DETERMINATION

Feasibility Study

FEASIBILITY PROCESS:

Feasibility Studies conduct to initiate the design and building process and selecting the architects and other professionals to begin the project. They usually involve to clinch approvals for various aspects of the project from relevant agencies, sometimes zoning approvals and performing a variety of tests to determine the soil, rock, and water conditions at the site. It is also essential to find the extent to which site remediation measures are needed before beginning the construction (for example, cleanup of a brownfield site).

City or State agencies may acquire a land that needs extensive site work because the property is less costly than other locations. Despite these issues, the property may offer some unique advantages as well. For example, they may be in sensible and influential spaces. The feasibility study will reveal problems that affect the usability of the building and required efforts and, cost to build the approved project.
Therefore, the clients and city agencies ensure that the Feasibility Study contract is forwarded to the architects, planners, engineers and other relevant experts.

In general, a **Feasibility Study involves the following steps** in the work process:

PROCESS

1. The process usually begins with a program review, including initial program strategies, site planning, and project cost requirements as well as the status of agency/city approvals.

DESIGN ASPECTS

2. Immediately, **the architect needs to assess the design context of emulating with the surrounding community,** the impact of sun and shade on program-use spaces, and the client's expectation for any advanced or specific design. A study of the local context of architecture will be particularly crucial if the nearby community resists the project. Therefore, it is essential to design a building of a style that will be well endowed by the surrounding community.

A study of the sun-path and orientation, at different times of the day to determine the placement and number of glazed surfaces and curtain walls or the need for a particular window shade system. These factors will also affect the project cost, so it is necessary to make the clients aware of them before the final selection of the site is confirmed.

Feasibility Study

SITE CONDITIONS

3. **Subsurface tests of soil conditions, contamination and groundwater conditions such as water table, flood zone category** will reveal the site's particular characteristics and related requirements. It is also necessary to study how the situations of surrounding sites affect the property under consideration (such as a water-flow from next to, on-site higher-level site area). These tests and their results may change project costs, time schedules, and further agency approvals.

4. The next step involves conducting a general study of the local drainage system, with dimensions of pipelines under the streets, as well as electrical and gas system layouts. These factors will affect the design of the drainage, electrical, and gas systems for the building and the time schedules for construction. This study will also help determine the interaction of the surrounding community with the proposed development aspects.

5. The surrounding area, buildings, views and impacting elements such as hills, water-bays, seas; all need to be reviewed, and determined about its effects related to the proposed project-building design.

CODE APPROVALS

6. **The Feasibility Study outlines the process for obtaining permits** and other approvals from the local city, state, or federal agencies to build a particular building on the property under consideration. It is essential to let the client know about the necessity of gaining these approvals. Without them, the project may come to a standstill and may result in a waste of time, money, and effort.

Learning to navigate the permit approval process may be considered as the first step toward establishing a professional practice. This skill will prove a valuable asset to the client and bolster the credibility of the architect. It is also essential to keep the client advised about the status of permits, especially in cases where the local community is resisting the project.

7. **The final step in the Feasibility Study may involve apprehension of the project and adjacent properties** to determine by a review, whether there is a need to replace the topsoil of the project site and the type of landscaping. It might be necessary to maintain air quality and help conserve building energy impact (heating, cooling, and lighting). In some cases, topsoil to a depth of a few feet needs to be replaced with better-quality soil, or existing trees may need to be uprooted entirely so that the designed landscape is not affected by pathogens that may have infested the existing vegetation.
Also, the architects and engineers could review the surrounding roadways and common areas to achieve a temporary possibility to deliver, store and process some handling of materials during the construction stage.

Finally, the site could be reviewed for particular security requirements, which might also affect the landscape. This analysis should be included in the project budget.

Feasibility Study

To go forward with a successful project, with advanced design, and project schedule, the architects, designers, and consultants also need to consider how the issues discovered in the feasibility study will be resolved and followed during the next phase, starting with schematic design.

FEASIBILITY STUDY DETERMINATION BY THE CLIENT

A thorough Feasibility Study, conducted before preliminary and schematic design begins, will help the architects, designers, and consultants anticipate the magnitude of problems that may arise and make adequate provisions for dealing with them in the client's future agreement. Otherwise, the project may be burdened with a host of problems, whether early in schematic design or later in the design development phase. The clients, owners, and agencies require the fulfillment of several criteria for the completion of the feasibility study determination and contracts with the architects and consultants.

The criteria are as follows:

1. When the property is found to be usable, they should go forward with a quick planning phase to satisfy programmatic expectations, code approvals, budget costs, and schedules for the completion of design and construction documents as well as the building process of the forthcoming built-project.

2. **The contracts should include input and recommendation from consultants** related to code approvals and cost estimates. The architect should review all details of the calculation to ensure it covers extraordinary circumstances and such requirements as fixing the soil conditions or providing flood and earthquake protection.

3. **The clients should consider particular condition such as an architect's intent and recommendations of the building design** to achieve a unique programmatic plan that is realistic and satisfactory to meet the program and client's strategy. The architect should pursue a high-end marketing strategy related to specific projects such as significant hi-rise condominium buildings within known cities that may affect design approach during preliminary and schematic design phases.

Such criteria and other suggestions noted above would forward possibilities of gaining the professional practice related to inviting projects.

Feasibility Study

During the Feasibility Study process, one should review and research the surrounding views to preconceive the design excellence.

Also, an Urban Design, as an inter-disciplinary subject utilizes elements of many built environment professions, including a landscape architecture within and surrounding sites.

Request For Proposal

Request For Proposal   RFP

An RFP, a Request for Proposal, solicits proposals for hiring and establishing the contracts with the architects, engineers, and other professionals who will carry out the whole intention about a development of the project.

The RFP also has importance in confirming the architects' professional status as well as their determination of how to proceed with the project using their experience. All such intention verifies and supports the selection of the firms to go forward with the successful project.

Request For Proposal

Contents:

RFP CONTENTS:

REQUEST FOR PROPOSAL (RFP)

FIRM'S AVAILABILITY

ARCHITECT SELECTION—OVERALL QUALIFICATIONS

WORKING PROCESS AND SPECIALTY

FORTHCOMING WORKING PROJECT

CONSTRUCTION SUPERVISION

Request For Proposal

Request For Proposal:

RFP is a beginning challenge to emanate from the profession. Since it is a starting process of selections of the architects, many clients review firm's ability, experience, and staff related to the type of their projects. The RFP submission should communicate **how the architect's particular skill, knowledge, or attention to sensitive project issues will enhance and improve the development of the client's project.** This review provides the focus of the Request for Proposal / RFP. The client may check the architects' references, the firm's status and then proceed with a meeting for final selections.

FIRM'S AVAILABILITY

If the first-selected firm is not available within a reasonable time for completion of the project, even with an acceptable fee status or for some other professional facet, the client can choose the second or third desired RFP received from other architects.

ARCHITECT'S SELECTION - OVERALL QUALIFICATIONS:

It is usually necessary to submit an RFP digitally and in a paper document format sent in a sealed envelope. The response should be in proper bullet points, essential items for discussions and the working arrangements. The content may vary depending on the project, but most submissions need short recommendations about planning, a site review, comments on assumed programming, fee amount, a timeline of completion of the project, **and a statement of why the architect/firm is most pertinent for preceding the project.** It should also include the firm's prior experience on similar type and affluent projects and their legal status in the profession.

To be ready to issue RFPs quickly, the architects should maintain up-to-date information on all projects, including substantial or specialized aspects of the projects and all references such as photographs, client letters noting the project's success, publications, and budget reviews.

RFP selection is best lowest; therefore, just the minimum fee may not always be the deciding factor by the client. Experience, professional references, and other backup information are also considered during selection. If the client states and expects a minimum fee, professionals may limit or adjust their scope of services. Unfortunately, this tends to add issues later about change orders by the contractors because of less achievement of necessary details or completion of the documents. **The architects should explain how their fees are related to the full scope of their work.** Then the client can select the architect not necessarily with the lowest fee-related issues or the fee amount. This process is, of course, complicated for the client to proceed with, but it ameliorates the results of handling the project.

Request For Proposal

WORKING PROCESS & SPECIALTY:

As a detailed version of an RFP for a renovation project can be included with specific items as described below:
Extreme or normal condition and stability of the exterior walls, floors, interior walls, doors, windows, ceilings, mechanical, electrical and all other types of building related items are crucial. As far as expanding, fixing, stabilizing these issues and existing conditions to provide the conversion of a building as an advanced and usable new school, office, residential, theater or any other type of building, all items should be proposed and included in the RFP description.

FORTHCOMING WORKING PROJECT:

Understanding the noted items below, the client could update their final decisions to select the architect for working on their project.

Management Proposal: The following items may be added to an RFP to encourage the client to think about this RFP selection approach to proceed with their project representing the unique creation of architecture. The purpose is to continue with active approvals by the client regarding, in general, the existing site and building study. The architects could suggest weekly meetings to keep the program, schedule, and budget on track; positively directing towards appropriate program design and schedule for completion of design and building construction of new building projects as well as possible alterations or renovations of for the existing building.

Later on, while another work process is going on, the architect should continue to check estimates so that the designed building will be within the budgeted estimate and construction schedule limits. The architect may try to gain code approvals before completion of the schematic design for anticipated problems and proposed solutions to the site and building conditions as described above while proceeding with finalizing the schematic layout.

The planning decisions must be coordinated and approved by the client to go forward with completion of the schematic design. Other technical conditions of the building process and construction may affect general planning, budget estimating, and the period for completion. **All of the above items provide evidence of how the architect will execute a prosperous project; to be explained in the RFP submission with desirable fee estimates.**

Although essential architectural practice should concentrate and find the correctly required elements to complete the final construction status of the projects, the architect should recommend the client in the RFP document to include their practical support to check individual building elements and suggestions related to the forthcoming specific site supervision. **All items shall be added in the RFP submission and should be recommended to the client.**

Request For Proposal

CONSTRUCTION SUPERVISION

Before submitting the RFP submission, **the architects should seek or ask about required site supervision status** because its use depends on the client side and their version as to what their project would need monitoring and checking the quality and installation of the materials. As evidence, **the clients may have their inspectors,** especially when they are from the same professional city agencies.

Although essential architectural practice should concentrate and find the factually required elements to complete the final construction status of the projects, the architect should recommend the client with their own practical support to check individual building elements and suggestions related to the forthcoming specific site supervision. **All of the above items shall be included in the RFP and should be recommended to the client.**

In essence, any Architect needs to informally explain the clients about the full completion of the projects with the necessity of attending towards all professional requirements to support gaining successful projects in the cities and countries.

Request For Proposal -Beginning of the project with the following initial process

Zoning Analysis, Usage, and Space Studies with Conclusions:

It is required to study the zoning analysis, given program accommodation on the site, or any waiver related to any particular use permit. Zoning analysis should include needed setbacks, maximum possible floor areas (mainly on the small sites in central city locations) and allowable heights.

Zoning Map:

Such presentation could express the surrounding areas for access to the sites, and travel units to reach the place as planned or required to meet the program.

Site Analysis and Approach:

It is vital to determine and confirm the site dimensions, location, access routes, construction workspaces, relative access sometimes along with the surrounding properties and connections with the program usage of the proposed building project.

Besides, the neighborhood area, types of buildings and the community access to those areas should be reviewed and discussed with the client and the neighbors as required by the community but should be processed by the architect during their design process.

Program study:

To start the design process, typically the architects need to review the program requirements in a detailed version. Any questions related to the various spaces and their usage if connected with the similar rooms should be clarified via meetings with the clients.

Program Diagrams:

To prepare Program Diagrams mainly establishing in general the widths and lengths related to the clients' intentions to use the spaces. However, as a particular effort, the architects could create and suggest the high-end usage formats of the areas indicating the recommended dimensions too.

Building Design Process:

The review, analysis of the program areas, and its relationship with the neighborhood character is an imperative process as a beginning of the building design. Further site approach towards the design features is explained on the next pages to help the designers to continue with their working process.

Schematic Design

Schematic Design

Schematic design is an initial design scheme for a project possibly based on preliminary design as an initial part of the action by architects and other professionals. This phase seeks to capture the client's expectations and intentions for the project as well as confirm such concrete issues as budget estimates and the bidding process. It is also an opportunity to present the project plans and design to the community and receive feedback on its potential impact and their support to establish the project decisions.

During this process, the clients need to endorse their opinions, confirmation of the program intended correctly and if applicable, per the current 21st century status as well as basic needs of the users.

Schematic Design

Contents:

PRE-CONCEPTION OF THE SCHEMATIC DESIGN

PRELIMINARY DESIGN

APPLICATION OF THE PRELIMINARY DESIGN

SITE AND PROPERTY PLANNING

SCHEMATIC DESIGN PROCESS

CLIENTS' STRATEGY AND FLOOR PLANNING

FLOOR PLANNING

EXTERIOR DESIGN

WORKING MODELS

CLIENT REACTIONS

BUDGET ESTIMATES

Schematic design

1. PRE-CONCEPTION OF THE SCHEMATIC DESIGN

As a process of dealing with medium to large projects, most of the time, it is recommended that architects integrate a *preliminary design phase* in their schematic design process. **The purpose is to encourage the pre-conception of a schematic design** that will develop the planning later in an acceptable and favorable direction. Although the clients may not recognize preliminary design as a contract phase, architects are encouraged to follow this step in their design process. A thorough preliminary design phase will help ensure an active schematic design phase.

Preliminary Design: Preconception of the handicapped access to the apartment buildings; with one, two and three entrances. (My work with Misra & Associates, PC, New York, NY. Owner-NYCHA)

The above site with landscape design, ADA planning and diagrams present the advanced intention to succeed with the happiness of the living status in the apartment buildings shown around. Such creation helps the residents to be attracted to their daily entertaining life status.

PRELIMINARY DESIGN: What is a preliminary design?

An influential opportunity initiates the importance and the purpose of the project to interact with the users and the surrounding community.

The preliminary designer starts with giving shape and form to the client's early expectations about the project. It considers whether the architectural style will be formal or not so formal, classical, historical, industrial, educational, cultural, Western or Eastern style. Preliminary design helps form a vision of the excellent results. This design will be too general at the beginning compared to the professional and practical expectations of the final project. However, an active phase of preliminary design may help meet the professional and realistic expectations of the project and by the communities as well.

Schematic design

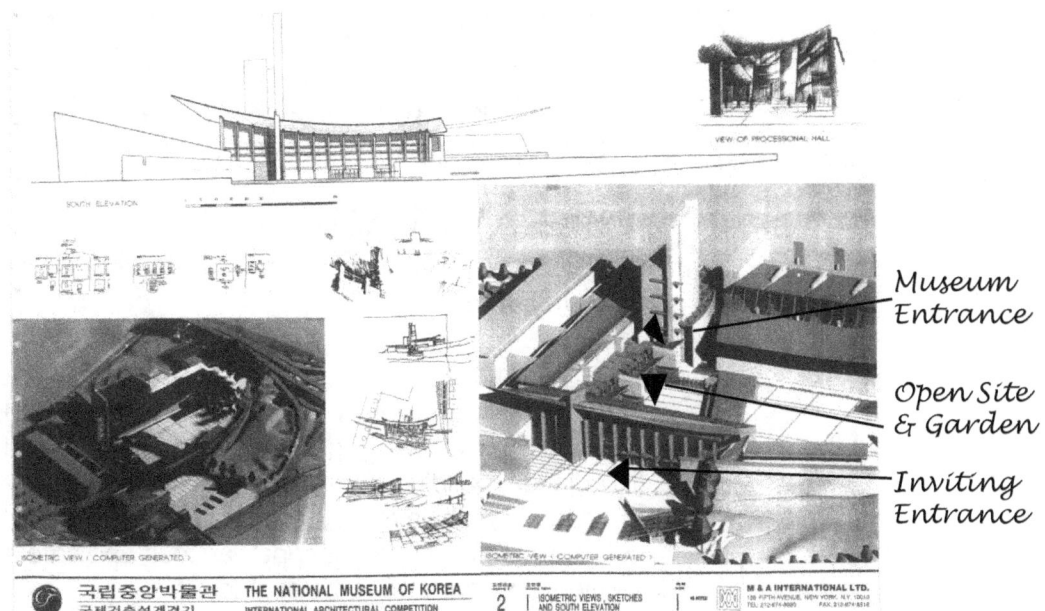

Korean Museum Design Competition: At Misra & Associates, PC, New York, NY. - Our sketches were the guidance in design. (My direction and management of the project in the firm)

2. APPLICATION OF THE PRELIMINARY DESIGN

In essence, *the preliminary design* includes ideas, goals, and intentions for the schematic design. **As an example of the initial design process, the above diagrams, drawings, and perspective views were related to Koreans' mainstream living standards and their life visions.** First, they pass through an inviting entrance space, then proceed to an open site and garden area, followed by the museum spaces beyond. This assumption is an example of an initial procedure of development of the schematic design process.

The question is, how would you want to lead your imagination?

Initially, the review and confirmation of the client's program requirements should be thoroughly examined and considered as the usability of the project. If the planning, designing, composition, adjustments of building plans, heights, entrances, and orientations are done skillfully, appropriately and are agreeable with the clients, then designers/architects will proceed with proper schematic design and garner overall approvals of the clients.

The methodology described above should be reviewed, compared with options, and discussed with the clients, city and state agencies, and the surrounding communities. In some projects, the process should also include the informed intentions of developers, marketing procedures, and the realistic involvement of specific countries, if applicable to the project. If the architect overlooks any of the factors related to the site and program requests, it is possible that his or her lack of foresight may be brought up by the client or the agency after much time is spent during the design process. **It is of particular importance for the architect to consider all factors in the design process;** otherwise, the result will be apparent in the initial presentation of the schematic design plans and views of the building or models, leading people to question the design intention.

Schematic design

3. TO BEGIN THE PRELIMINARY DESIGN:

A preliminary design process includes the following steps:
Here is a primary method one can start the design process:

SITE APPROACH:
REVIEW THE PROJECT WITH SURROUNDING COMMUNITY BUILDINGS.

1. *Visit the site to study immediately,* **the surrounding buildings and community user areas such as urban parks. It is also important to note the following**: ground elevations, sun path, shadows cast by existing adjacent buildings if around, views to and from existing buildings and the site, roads or highways leading towards the site. And the main entrance location, the suitability of handicapped access and safe entry area from busy roads or highways are also to be evaluated.

Such new commercial building plans with significant spaces facing entrance and lobby should be inviting the arranged community and the building users around. Regarding other projects too, it is vital to indicate and study the surrounding views and availability to enter the site to access the main entrance. Depending upon the type of projects, the site area near the entrances may be used as entry roads for cars and reaching toward the accessible outdoor ramps for the handicapped/disabled persons' usability.

SITE AND PROPERTY PLANNING -Site Diagram - Landscape & Water issues

The surrounding landscape and the building designs are always inviting the owners and their friends to reach the place.

The architect must study the site, taking into consideration existing healthy and good- quality trees. Examples of this would be, creating access paths towards the entrance through rows of trees and arranging proper locations of car parking spaces and areas around, with shrubs and trees. Some trees provide shade and good design for reasonable exposure to the sunshine /hot weather and reducing unattractive view impacts of empty ground areas. However, while planning, it is essential to study the growth rate and direction of the roots of the existing trees, as they would affect the excavations, construction of the foundations, footings and the ground slabs for parking spaces and, its ground level building in the same area.

1. **Existing natural landscapes**, such as a row of evergreen trees along the edge of the site, can provide privacy and protection. Trees and other healthy vegetation can help address a variety of site issues: directing pedestrian or vehicle movement; framing vistas; creating shade and glare wind protection and reducing stormwater runoff.

2. **Acoustical event detection is** necessary to consider and respond to the busy or noisy areas around, such as railroad tracks, highways, or manufacturing facilities. See item 8 on page 48, for some solutions to acoustical problems.

Schematic design

As an example, the layout shown below indicates four office buildings, which could be built as required either one building at a time or more, with the necessary numbers of the parking spaces and access roads. They are planned with central corridors, which could be connected if the buildings are for combined professional businesses.

Arranging proper locations of car parking spaces and areas with shrubs and trees around.

The main entrance locations

CC - Conference Center
C - Cafeteria
M - Media Center
O - Office

First building to start original program

Creating access paths towards the entrance through rows of trees

Roads or highways leading towards the site

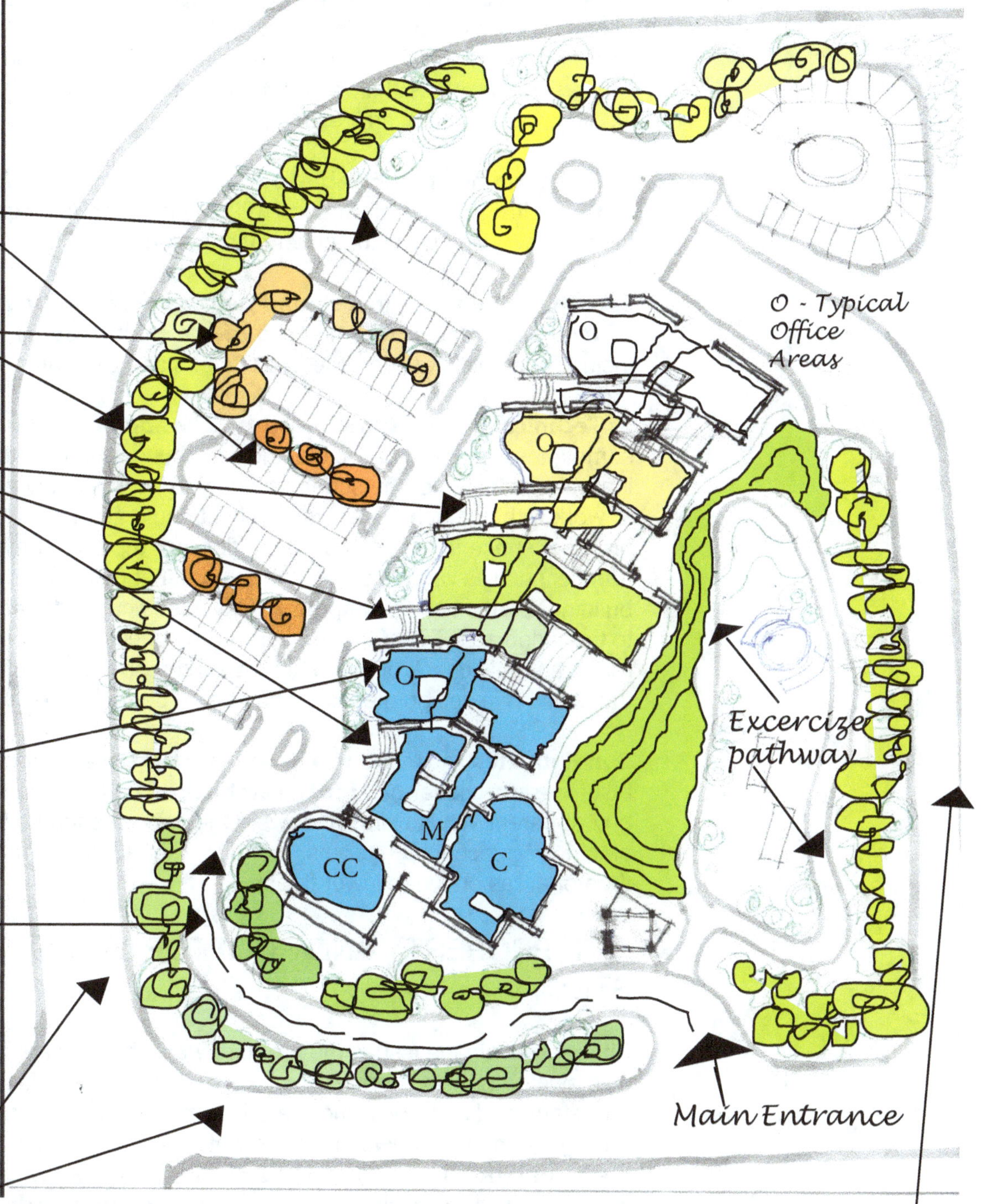

O - Typical Office Areas

Exercize pathway

Main Entrance

Backup road drive for material deliveries

SITE AND PROPERTY PLANNING PRELIMINARY DESIGN LAYOUT

Schematic design

4. TO FORWARD THE PRELIMINARY DESIGN: SETBACKS, HEIGHT LIMITS, AND BUILDING FOOTPRINT

1. **To review requirements for setbacks from the property lines,** as controlled by the town/city agencies: Entry and egress to and from the site are also important considerations, including the impact of adjacent properties on traffic flow and direction. Sometimes the egress drive required by the neighboring properties as well as their exit directions passing through the design property would need to remain as it exists.

2. **To determine the allowable footprint areas and the total allowable height of the building:** This information will be fundamental for general planning of all program spaces during the schematic design.

Each available floor area should be considered to be at least adding 25% of over the total program areas of the major rooms on the same floor to include wall-thicknesses, toilets, exit stairs and exit corridors. See page 31.

3. **Technical spaces should also be considered in the planning** although, sometimes, mechanical and electrical consultants cannot tell the architect about it at the beginning of the schematic design work as they do not have the plans to work with. In such case, the architect could add about 5 percent of the total program space to be used on each floor for the HVAC and electricity service-transfer such as vertical ducts, cables, water and plumbing pipes throughout the building. In addition to that, the HVAC, electrical and mechanical rooms need to be added as 5-7% of the total program spaces. Such process leads towards real pragmatic check of the total required gross area automatically used during the schematic design planning and should be rechecked during next phases.

Building sites in dense urban areas with several adjacent tall buildings also present challenges for the architect. The lower five floors may not have any apparent views from windows. One way to address this issue is to place electrical/ mechanical rooms, service rooms, or gymnasium/exercise and theater areas on these lower floors.

SITE/PROPERTY AND ROOFTOP DRAINAGE SYSTEM STUDY

Sites with drainage issues may require water-holding areas to control outgoing wastewater in a city's drainage system. In the design development phase, the roof slabs and waterproofing materials may need to be conceived in a way to arrange them to hold two inches of water, for twenty-four hours on the rooftop. **Such condition is required because the drainage pipes under the streets are designed sometimes with smaller diameter dimensions than the standard necessary sizes.** The roof areas hold about two inches of water for a day allowing a reasonable but lesser amount of water through the drainage pipes under the streets to follow the function as planned by the city.
Such process may impact the height of the buildings because of the rooftop parapet wall heights.

Schematic design

Water pond stabilized in the ground with holding its connection to street water drainage for sometime as required by the city.

Total gross floor area could be considered to be added with at least 25 percent over the entire program areas of the major rooms. See below.

Such planning aspect could result quickly as a floor plan, room locations and, secondary required program areas. See below.

Rooftops- Need to have 2" high water holding area as secondary water space with scuppers.

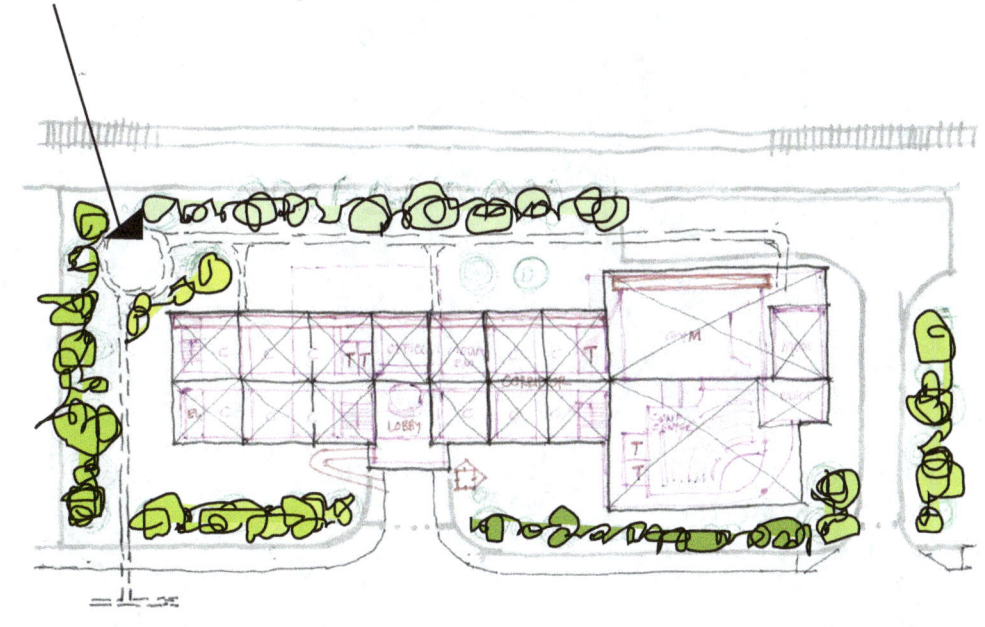

Preliminary Design Plan... A Public High School

C - Classroom
M - Media Center

Total gross floor area could be considered by adding at least 25 percent of the entire program areas of the major rooms.

Such planning could result quickly as a floor plan, room locations and, secondary required program areas such as restrooms, corridors, and exit stairs. These spaces could be located adjacent to the main program areas.

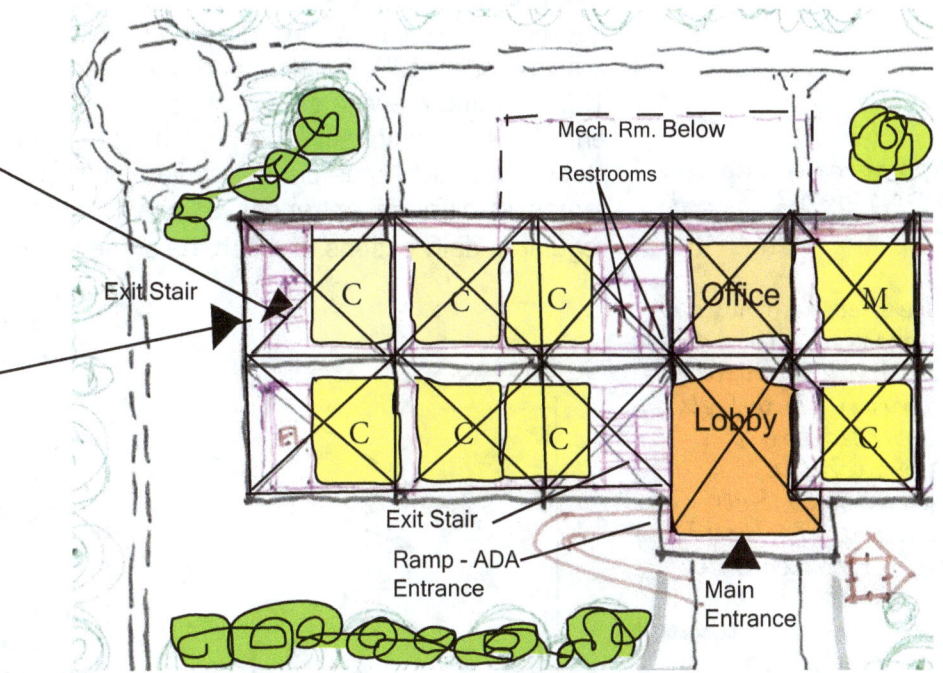

Preliminary Design - Quickly planned with program areas.

Schematic design

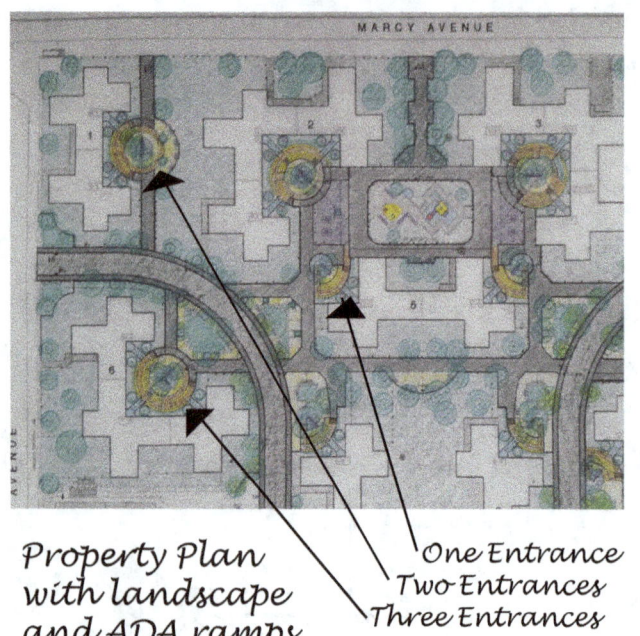

Property Plan with landscape and ADA ramps for varied entrances

One Entrance
Two Entrances
Three Entrances

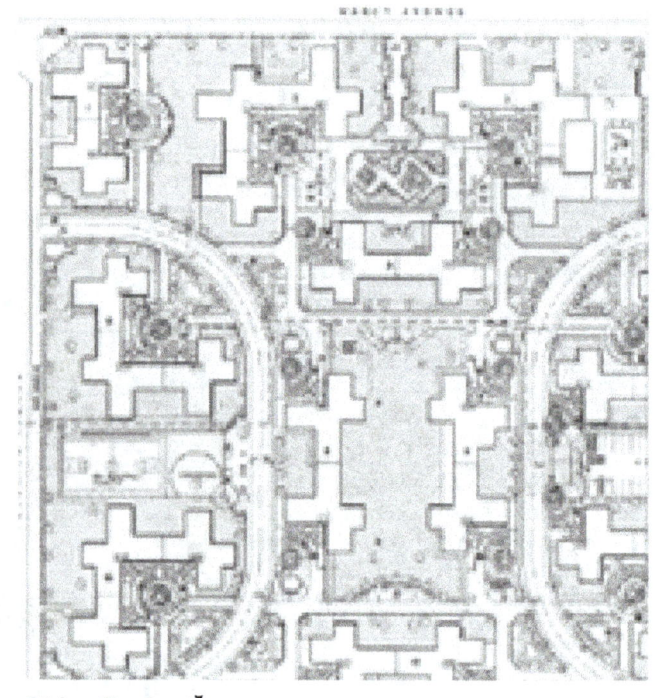

Site Detail

Entry and surrounding areas - Site Plan for the ADA Ramps and entrances - Owner- NYCHA (I had worked and created this project with Misra & Associates, PC, New York, NY)

5, SITE APPROACH: SCHEMATIC DESIGN PROCESS- ADA Entrance access to all buildings

Original site view

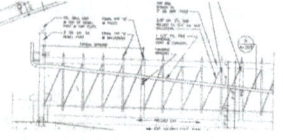

Typical railing design for less than 2'-6" high sloping ramp area.

As a design process, the architect could start thinking about how one comes in to reach the building elements. The designer should consider how one approaches the building and whether it is attractive while inviting the users. The following drawing shows an approach to a building with three ADA ramp-entrances. Intentionally, the circular ramps are adjacent so that the various slopes and lengths as planned adjacent to each other, can create the variable ramps at different entrances at site locations. Such design enhances their regular or daily actions to reach the same place.

The sketch shows an approach to their building. With such planning, one feels attracted to approach the entrance to their residential building and enhance their regular or daily actions, to go toward the same place.

Enjoying seating or devoting some routine daily actions before or after entering their apartments.

The design perfectly leads them towards the entry steps and the front portion may always initiate such entertainment within their life.

Access to their entrances after reaching and using the ADA ramps or the steps.

Entrance
Entrance
Entrance

Schematic design

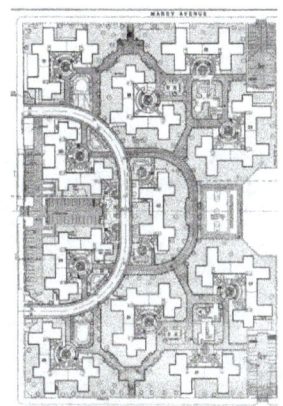

Half of the site area

ADA Ramps and three entrances (See plan on the page 32)
With steps to sit and enjoy the evenings with friends.

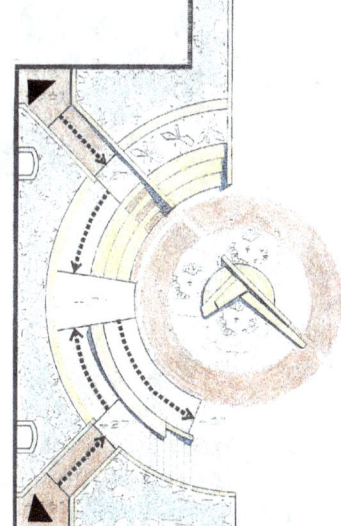

ADA Ramps and two entrances

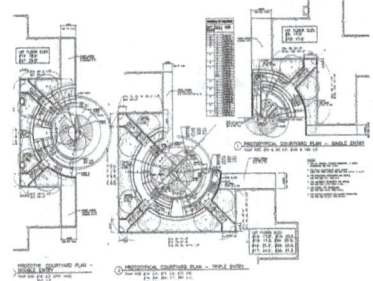

Plan Details - Working Drawings

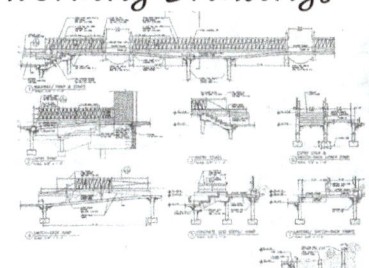

ADA Ramp and one entrance
with steps to sit and enjoy the evenings with friends.

Sections & Details   Original Existing Site & Landscape

Schematic design

Residential House – Type 1

Unfinished exterior landscape

RESIDENTIAL HOUSE: ENTRANCE REACHED BY VARIOUS INVITING STEPS AND SOMETIMES SEATING ON THE LOW SIDEWALLS TO WAIT FOR THEIR FRIENDS

6. CLIENTS' STRATEGY & FLOOR PLANNING

For example, **the design for the entrance to a house creates an inviting access for the owner's friends and family** while also reinforcing respect for their status as the friends. Their friends and other families visit the house as a large group, contributing the honor of the owner. Entering such a highly admired and inviting entrance achieves respecting the owner and shows politeness receiving their friends and guests.

Exterior Steps & Landings

Interior Stair

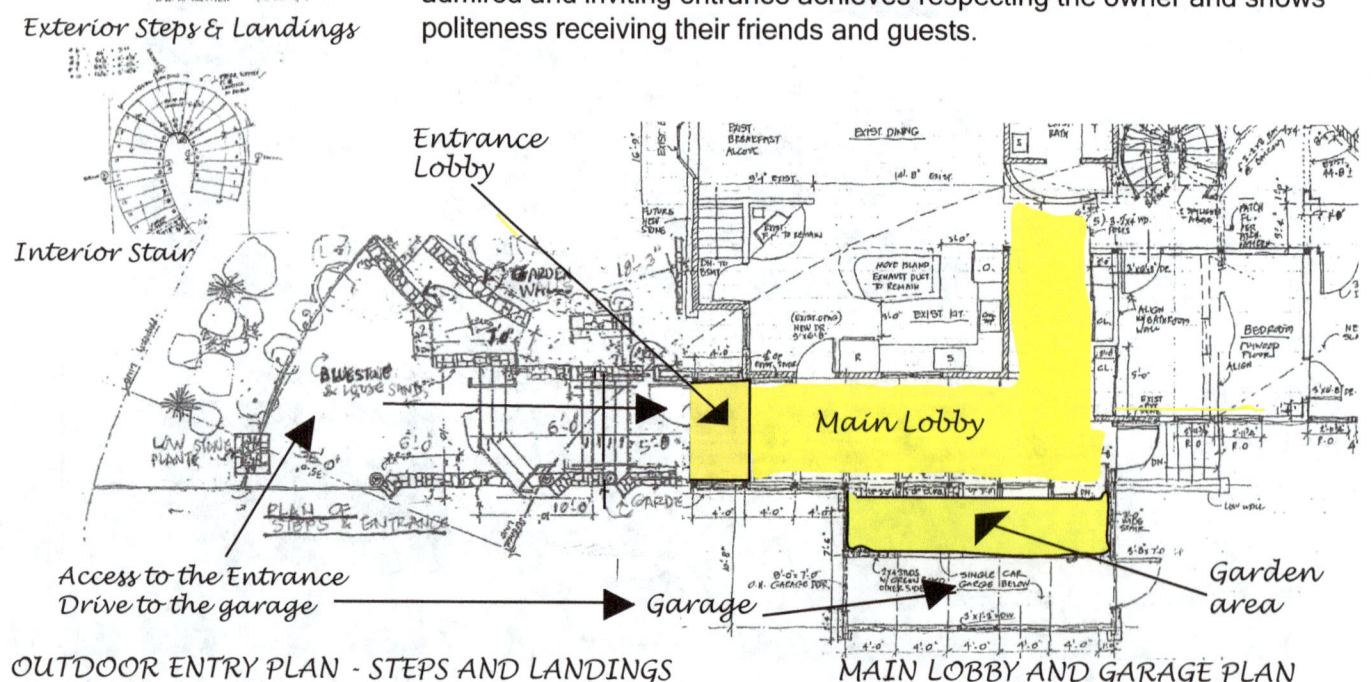

OUTDOOR ENTRY PLAN - STEPS AND LANDINGS   MAIN LOBBY AND GARAGE PLAN

Schematic design

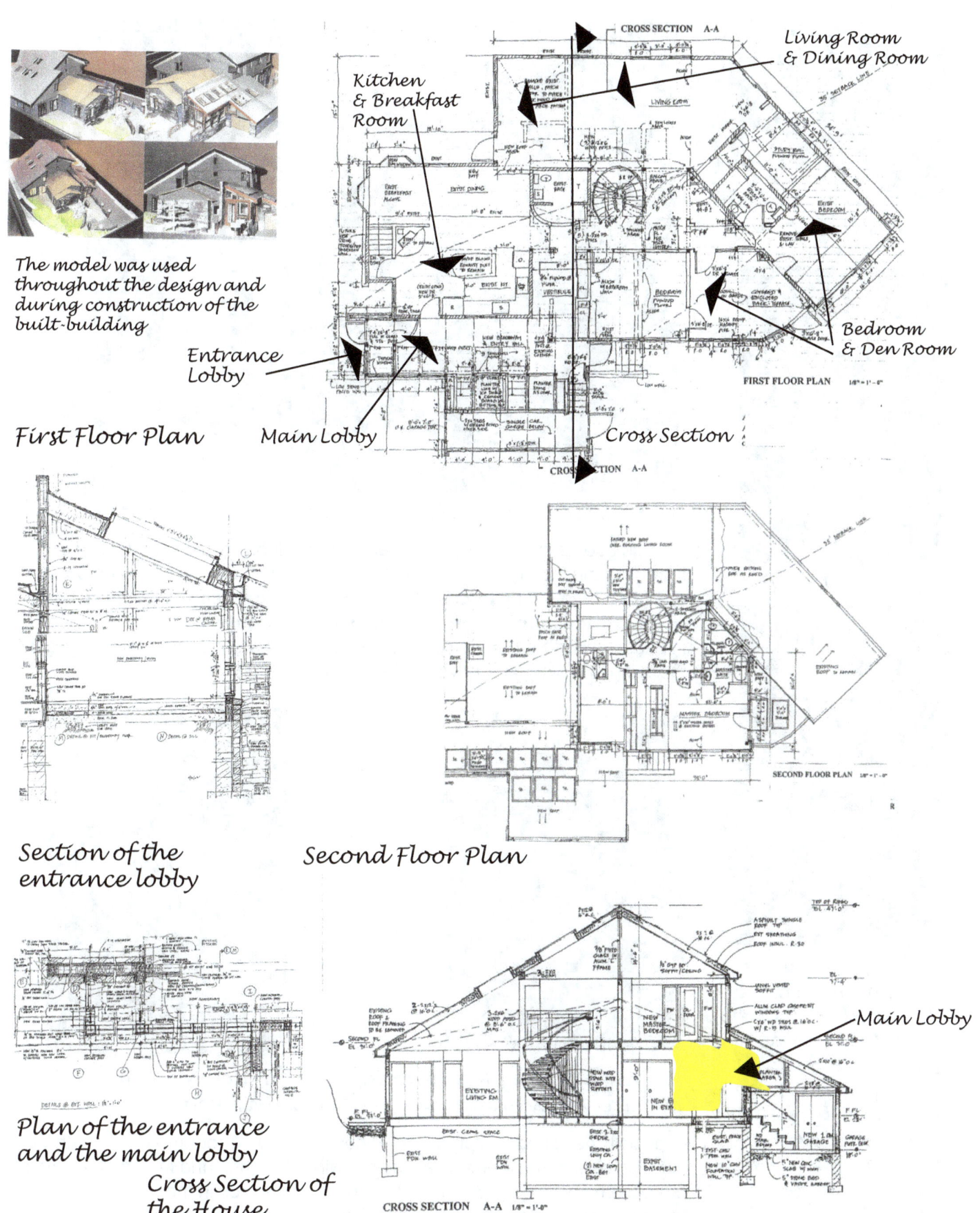

The model was used throughout the design and during construction of the built-building

First Floor Plan

Section of the entrance lobby

Plan of the entrance and the main lobby

Kitchen & Breakfast Room

Living Room & Dining Room

Entrance Lobby

Bedroom & Den Room

Main Lobby

Cross Section

Second Floor Plan

Cross Section of the House

Main Lobby

Schematic design

Main Lobby with a garden space

Sculptural Wall

RESIDENTIAL HOUSE TYPE 1: ENTRANCE AND MAIN LOBBY

1. The guests enter through a small entrance lobby that prevents cold air from entering the house and then they proceed into the main interior lobby and other rooms. **The interior lobby features a garden space where the guest introductions are exchanged with each other**, and coats are stored in beautiful closets. As they continue to the living room, they may not imagine the living and dining room views they will encounter.

Going forward through a specially designed sculptural wall, then it was a surprise looking at 23' high living room ceiling height with a museum-style picture-walls, skylights, and the nearby dining room.

23' High Living Room Height and Museum style picture walls on one side of the living room

A specially designed sculptural wall leads to the living room with twenty-three-foot-high ceiling, museum-style picture walls, skylights, and the nearby dining room. Such design process grasps client's living status in their house. Additional view of this 23' high Living Room is shown on page 50.

Schematic design

Residential House Type 1

The renovated house now looks as if it belongs in this neighborhood as well as an inviting place for guests and neighbors.

Stair climbing towards the upper bedrooms

Such distinctive design of the stair was managed by correctly locating each supporting steel tubes, the layout of each step and later, the 12" and 16" long stainless steel tubes as the curved-hand-railings arrangement, installed as shown. With such design effort and construction process arranged by Kala, the total estimated cost of the stair was reduced from $ 20,000 to $ 8,000. Previously, the existing house did not have any access-stair inside, since it was only a ground floor building.

Previously, the existing house was barely visible from the surrounding million dollar homes. After it had been redesigned and built, as shown above, it was treated as a respectful version in the neighborhood.

In-house stair to reach the master bedroom and second bedroom. It also promotes and presents the owner reaching down towards the living room to welcome their guests to parties.

Living room

Schematic design

During schematic design, if the lobby has to advocate some requirements, such as wall-planning, with a proper welcoming and inviting style information, it is vital to create such plan. It is important to arrange and pursue to provide a floor space or wall area for interior design presentation with objects representing the results of the business achievements.

OFFICE BUILDINGS - ENTRANCE LOBBIES
CLIENTS ACHIEVEMENTS SHOWN AS PAINTINGS TO SUPPORT AND INFORM ABOUT THEIR BUSINESS INTENTIONS AND RESULTS

ENTRANCE LOBBIES AND SURROUNDING AREA- OFFICE BUILDING

2. Depending on the type of professional/business projects, the space near the entrance will be used for parking and arrivals by car, as well as handicapped access ramps.

Then when one enters the main lobby, the person is directed to the stairs, elevators, reception desks, security guard areas, and perhaps some small offices. **Besides, certain lobbies may have typical visual impacts** such as shown in the above sketches with the presentation of some admired paintings and pictures **as planned work by the client in their business.**

a. The entrance issues require available sufficient area on the main floor with spaces necessary to be near the entrances as listed above and below.

b. In some cases, the exit stairs may end up in the lobby as well if the exterior doors are wide enough for exit dimensions. In most projects, lobby walls, doors, and ceilings must be fire rated to 1 1/2 hours. See page 54.

c. Beyond the reception desks, some of the office areas and contact spaces should be designed to direct people toward the main active spaces such as theater entrances, conference halls, media rooms, public restrooms, and a snack or drink supply-stores.

d. Based on the type of buildings – schools, theaters, museums, libraries, or residential buildings – **there are various strategies to be considered when planning the upper and lower floors**. These procedures are discussed below in items 4 and 5 on the page 39 and 41.

Schematic design

3. To succeed in the process of schematic design, an architect should study the site footprint at the first-or ground-floor plan. In this process, **it is critical to review the required setbacks from the property lines and the allowable planning-sizes at every floor level, sometimes needed as a percentage of the property area.** The maximum height of the building will control the number of floors/levels as well as the allowable floor plan area. Such planning is one of the processes of finalizing the required and available gross area.

4. **In urban areas, window placement and views are critical to consider in the planning** of the commercial office/business buildings especially in meeting and conference rooms as well as rooftop presentation and observation areas. It is achieved by considering other influencing factors such as the window locations toward the visible sites or above the adjacent buildings towards the beautiful surrounding area. In residential projects, most rooms should lead towards exterior views. Such process finally advises the clients and implements visitors' appreciation of using those spaces every day.

Similar planning for the upper floors and the below ground levels should continue. It is important to remember that the intentions and decisions of the design would serve realistic expectations of the client.

Below is the result of the initial processing an architect can use, to begin preliminary design. With such process, the architect would have in general, an idea of how the whole planning of the building could be turned as, theoretical, practical, and an award-winning/high-end design version. **As related to the office building planning shown on page 29, the following sketch shows the first office building plan connected with additional office buildings beyond.**

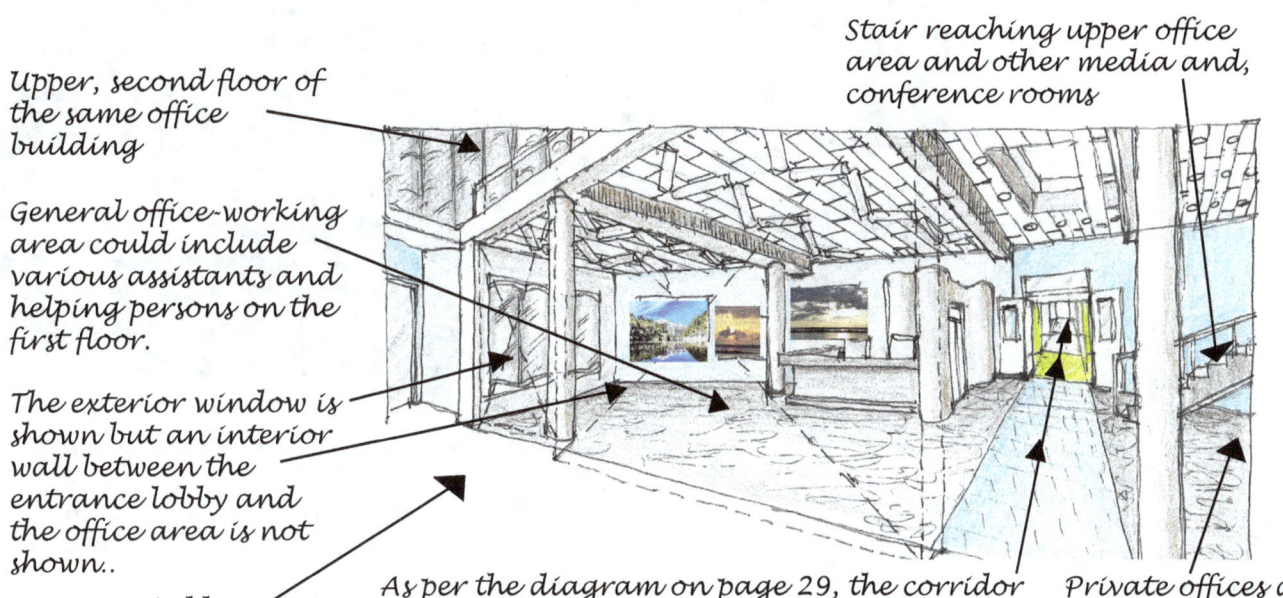

Upper, second floor of the same office building

General office-working area could include various assistants and helping persons on the first floor.

The exterior window is shown but an interior wall between the entrance lobby and the office area is not shown..

Entrance Lobby

Stair reaching upper office area and other media and, conference rooms

Private offices and conference area

As per the diagram on page 29, the corridor could be extended towards further office buildings, to be connected with each other.

A preliminary design of the first office building area as shown on page 29.

Schematic design

RESIDENTIAL HOUSE
TYPE 1

THE RENOVATED HOUSE

Finally presented an ultimate success regarding its status to be in surrounding million dollar homes as well as an inviting place for guests and neighbors.

House Model and front view of construction building

New Residential completed House

A Detail section of the entrance lobby is shown on page no. 35

Preliminary Design

ADVANCED DESIGN:
Starting with the preliminary design, the architect, in general, need to have an idea of how the whole planning of the building could be practical, theoretical, and an award-winning/high-end design version.

By proceeding with the models and the practical approach to update the planning status, it resulted in an appreciated version of a new house.

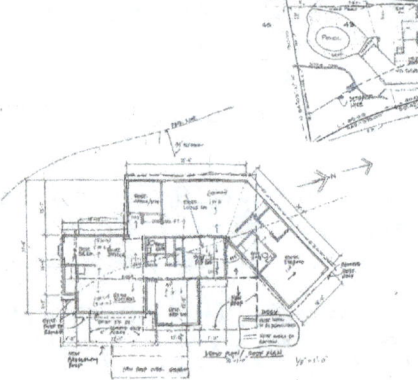

EXISTING HOUSE:
Originally, the house was created as a basic usable plan but with minimum caliber in the surrounding admired site with other beautiful homes.

Previously, the existing house was barely visible from the surrounding site area with other million dollar homes.

Schematic design

5. Window placement will influence the planning of program spaces. **Since the visibility outside the windows makes a significant difference, it is automatically an influencing factor in the preparation of the program areas and locations of superior rooms and forms.** Designing the building project with these factors will help enhance the overall schematic design phase. Therefore, the architect should already have the adjoining pictures even before starting the schematic design layout.

SURROUNDING AREA AND VIEWS

As shown below, the condominiums are set up at locations where the views-shown below are visional every day.
Therefore, the architect has planned all condominium units to be able to let the owners see the similar view through their rooms.

As a result, it is known as a very appropriate marketing value for all units and owners.

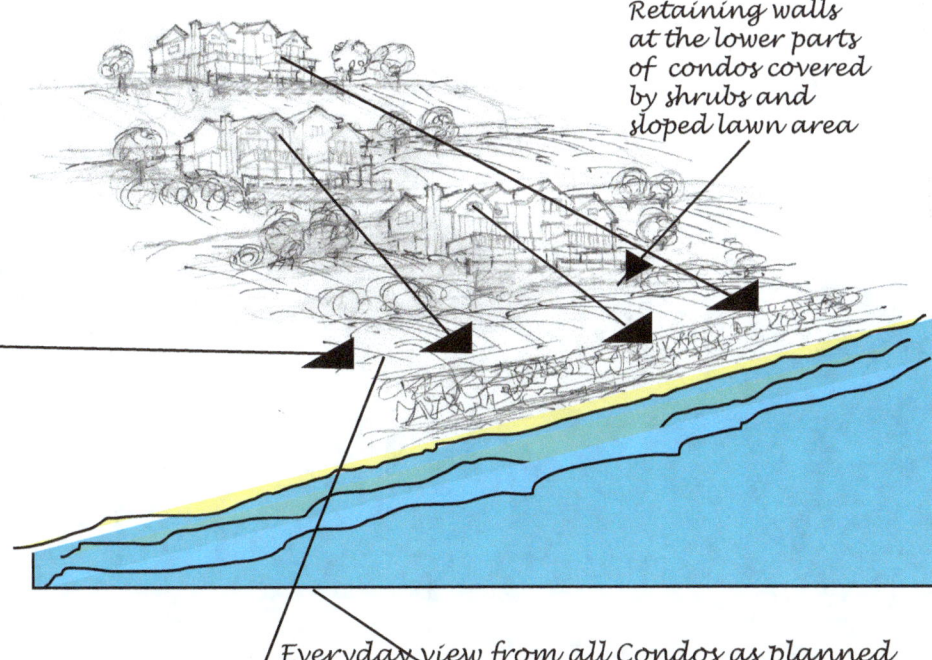

Retaining walls at the lower parts of condos covered by shrubs and sloped lawn area

Everyday view from all Condos as planned

Daily contiguous views from all condominiums as a part of the successful design

Schematic design

New Residential House - Type 2

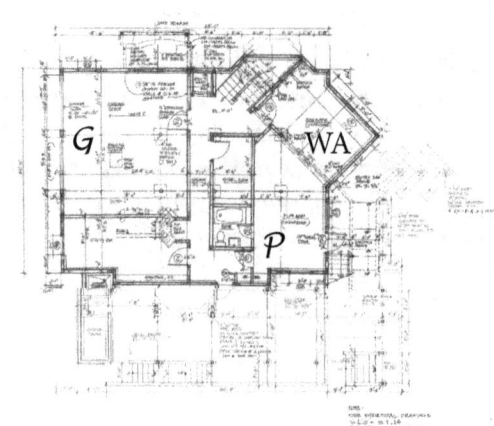

G - Garage

WA - Work Area

P - Playroom

Ground Floor Plan: Provides access to the primary and secondary entrance upward to reach the main first floor rooms. This ground floor has children's playrooms, and other workable areas.

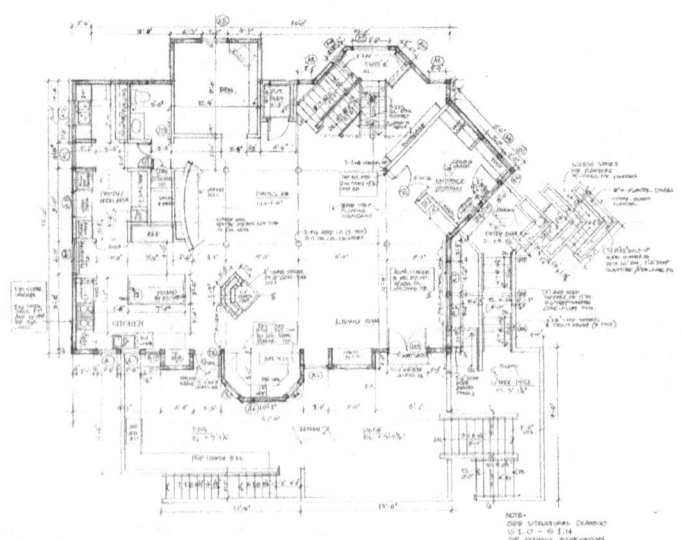

First floor plan - See Page 43

Second Floor plan

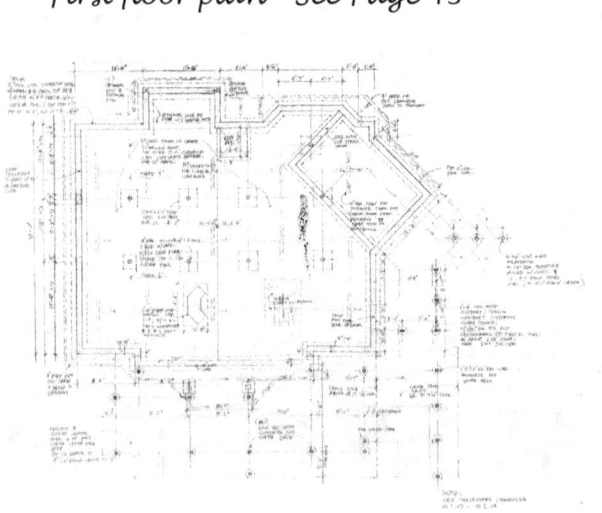

One can create a working model showing the general plan layouts and imagining an exterior design to achieve the highest quality of planning. See page nos. 43 and 51.

Foundation plan: Depending on the location near a large water bay such building foundations should be with piles or much deeper and suitable foundations.

Schematic design

BR. - Bed Rooms above

DK. Deck

DR. - Den room

D - Dining Area

K. - Kitchen

L. - Living room area

LR - Library

P. - Pantry

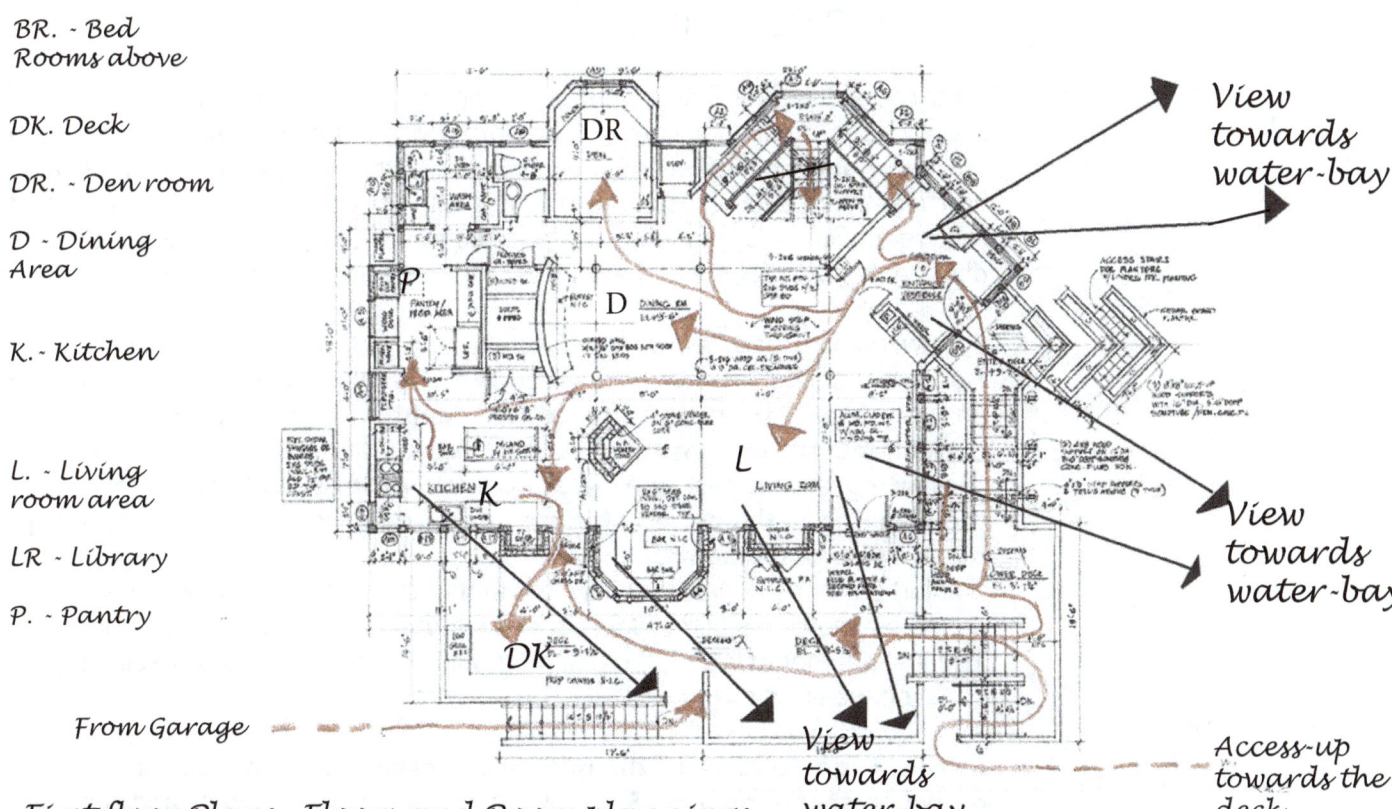

View towards water-bay

View towards water-bay

View towards water-bay

From Garage

Access-up towards the deck

First floor Plan: Floors and Room planning: Related to and from, room-to-access room location. Similar design for the upper floors and the below-ground levels should be continued. It is important to remember that the intentions and decisions of the design would serve realistic expectations of the client.

S-E Elevation- View towards water-bay.

working model

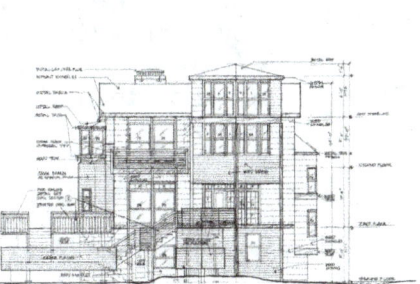

N-E Elevation- View towards water-bay.

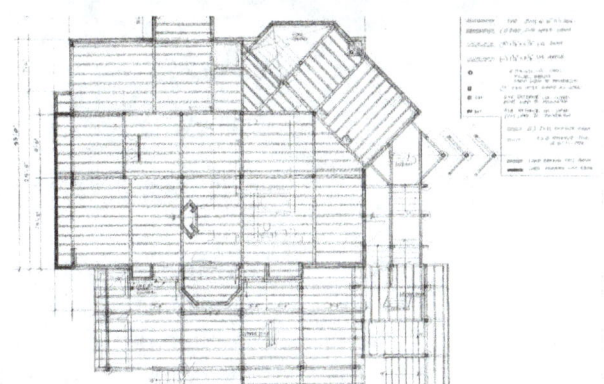

Structural plan: First floor slab.

Schematic design

7. FLOOR PLANNING

After conducting the above study, the impact of the surrounding areas at the site location, finding acceptable heights, and footprints, **the architect can start working on single-line room plans on various floors.** They must also consider the relationships of these rooms with the convenient connections that require a suitable approach and proper communication possibilities within the different types of rooms, departments, and meeting or conference rooms.

- Lower floors and belowground levels may provide ideal locations for the placement of the main project supports and service rooms for the high-rise building project. **Using the suggestions mentioned on page 31 regarding the community-use, an architect can quickly plan a single-line layout in presenting the highest quality, status, and professional results regarding the planning of the projects before further detailing the schematic design plans and arrangements.**

To start a program layout, initially, the architect can create some scaled diagrams showing all program spaces as a group of the same usage units. The first attempt to initiate the planning will be fast-forwarded by assigning some shapes and sizes.

At this stage, to forward the quality of design, one can create a working model presented on page 51, showing the general plan layouts and imagined exterior design. This medium is the exact opportunity to produce the highest level of design results and receives the client's approvals and comments as well as those of other partners and designers in the firm. Along with such process, the architect can arrange and schedule meetings with the city agencies to start the process of their initial comments related to further approvals.

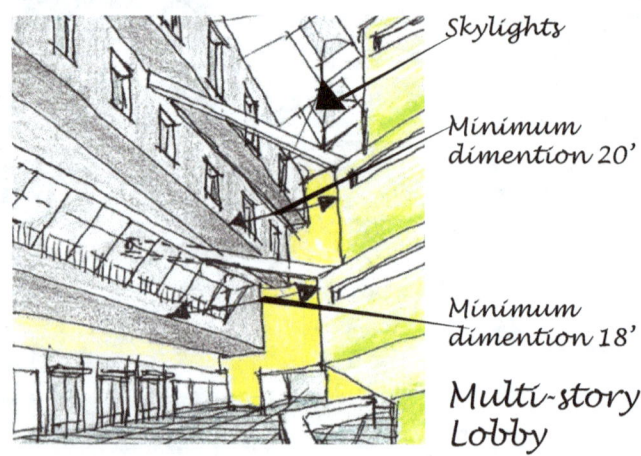

Skylights

Minimum dimention 20'

Minimum dimention 18'

Multi-story Lobby

For example, a high entrance lobby with the narrow width may be approved as a multi-story lobby rather than an Atrium (which has to be the minimum of 44' wide). Such special City-approvals advance the result of the completed building.

STRUCTURAL PLANNING

- **Using the geotechnical report** indicating soil conditions, groundwater conditions as well as the intended upper and underground planned spaces, the architectural design should advocate the decisions about the type of structural design directions. **It applies to typical individual interior column foundations, continuous exterior wall and column foundations, piles at an impacted ground at specific properties next to water bays, etc.**

Schematic design

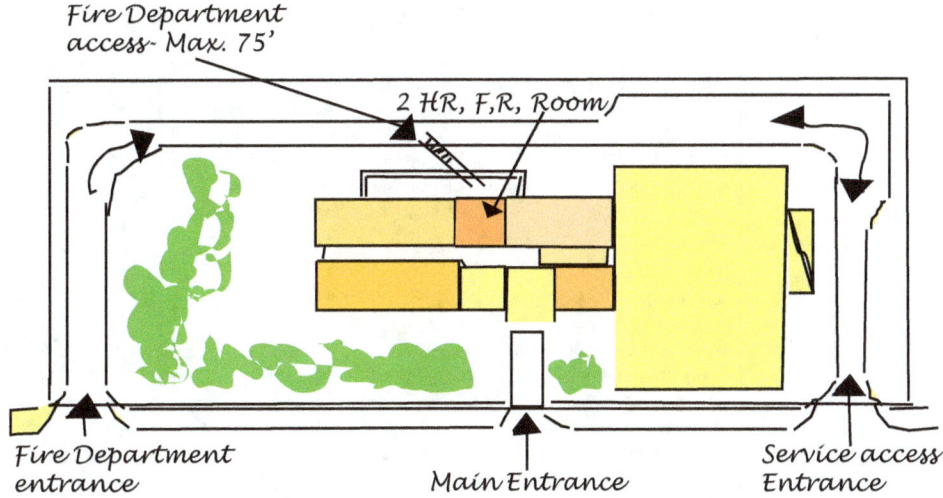

ROOFTOP EXIT DIRECTION WITH GENERAL REQUIREMENTS: The rooftop plan and the 2-hr. fire rated room for people exiting through upper floors towards outside as shown above.

FIRE DEPARTMENT ACCESS IF REQUIRED AND TO BE PLANNED

• **Tops of the buildings** have possibilities to install AC units and HVAC units. **Besides, the planning should include possible fire-resisting exit plans.** (Fire-exit situations besides the typical stair exits: If approved by the City, Town or State, an architect can design roofs with a certain height, such as a maximum of seventy-five feet and with accessible approaches by the fire departments to provide **fire-exit situations from the rooftops**.) It is known that at so many locations where the fire departments have protected and saved human beings by relieving them from the fire exposure by approaching the rooftops of buildings that are on top of the floors during the strength of the building.

• Such planning requires proper dimensions on the site, outside the same building property along the side streets to allow fire departments access along the property edges/lines and capture the access locations along the building exterior, windows, doors and other rooftop door access/exit areas reachable by using fire departments' ladders. In essence, to require the fire department process to proceed with fire safety, it requires a sufficient open, accessible area around the property.

Schematic design

PROJECT DEVELOPMENT & ORGANIZATION

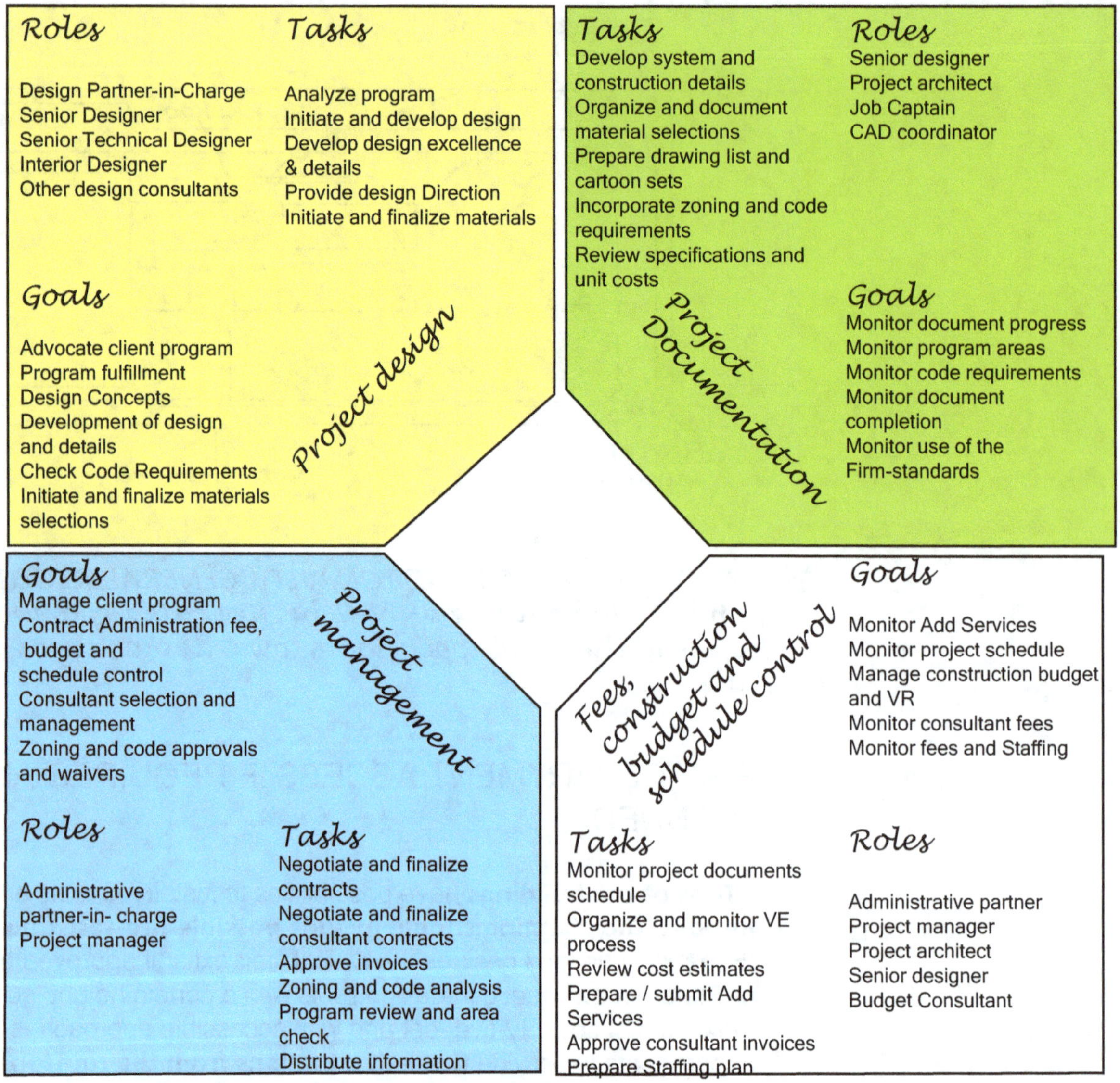

Project design

Roles
- Design Partner-in-Charge
- Senior Designer
- Senior Technical Designer
- Interior Designer
- Other design consultants

Tasks
- Analyze program
- Initiate and develop design
- Develop design excellence & details
- Provide design Direction
- Initiate and finalize materials

Goals
- Advocate client program
- Program fulfillment
- Design Concepts
- Development of design and details
- Check Code Requirements
- Initiate and finalize materials selections

Project Documentation

Tasks
- Develop system and construction details
- Organize and document material selections
- Prepare drawing list and cartoon sets
- Incorporate zoning and code requirements
- Review specifications and unit costs

Roles
- Senior designer
- Project architect
- Job Captain
- CAD coordinator

Goals
- Monitor document progress
- Monitor program areas
- Monitor code requirements
- Monitor document completion
- Monitor use of the Firm-standards

Project management

Goals
- Manage client program
- Contract Administration fee, budget and schedule control
- Consultant selection and management
- Zoning and code approvals and waivers

Roles
- Administrative partner-in-charge
- Project manager

Tasks
- Negotiate and finalize contracts
- Negotiate and finalize consultant contracts
- Approve invoices
- Zoning and code analysis
- Program review and area check
- Distribute information

Fees, construction budget and schedule control

Goals
- Monitor Add Services
- Monitor project schedule
- Manage construction budget and VR
- Monitor consultant fees
- Monitor fees and Staffing

Tasks
- Monitor project documents schedule
- Organize and monitor VE process
- Review cost estimates
- Prepare / submit Add Services
- Approve consultant invoices
- Prepare Staffing plan

Roles
- Administrative partner
- Project manager
- Project architect
- Senior designer
- Budget Consultant

The above chart explains a necessary arrangement in general for producing and organizing projects. Such information will forward a perspective regarding the determination of the team responsibilities and processing projects as well as a firm responsibility.

Sometimes some of the architects may need to know general information about a project development and organization related to the project design, project documentation, project management and, fees, construction budgets and project schedule.

Such knowledge leads the teams to process their responsibilities and later; they would be able to develop a further process to organize and carry on with new projects as per their known determinations.

Design & Documentation
Project Schedule

Specifically, handling a massive project and working with partners and many team members, it is very active to create a project schedule which could include and organize, preparations of the Clients' meetings, and required presentations of the documents. Later, other successful versions of project submissions, such as exterior wall dimensions and acoustical impact with positive results, project involvement related to contractors' expectations, and all city agencies' approvals should be indicated in the same schedule.

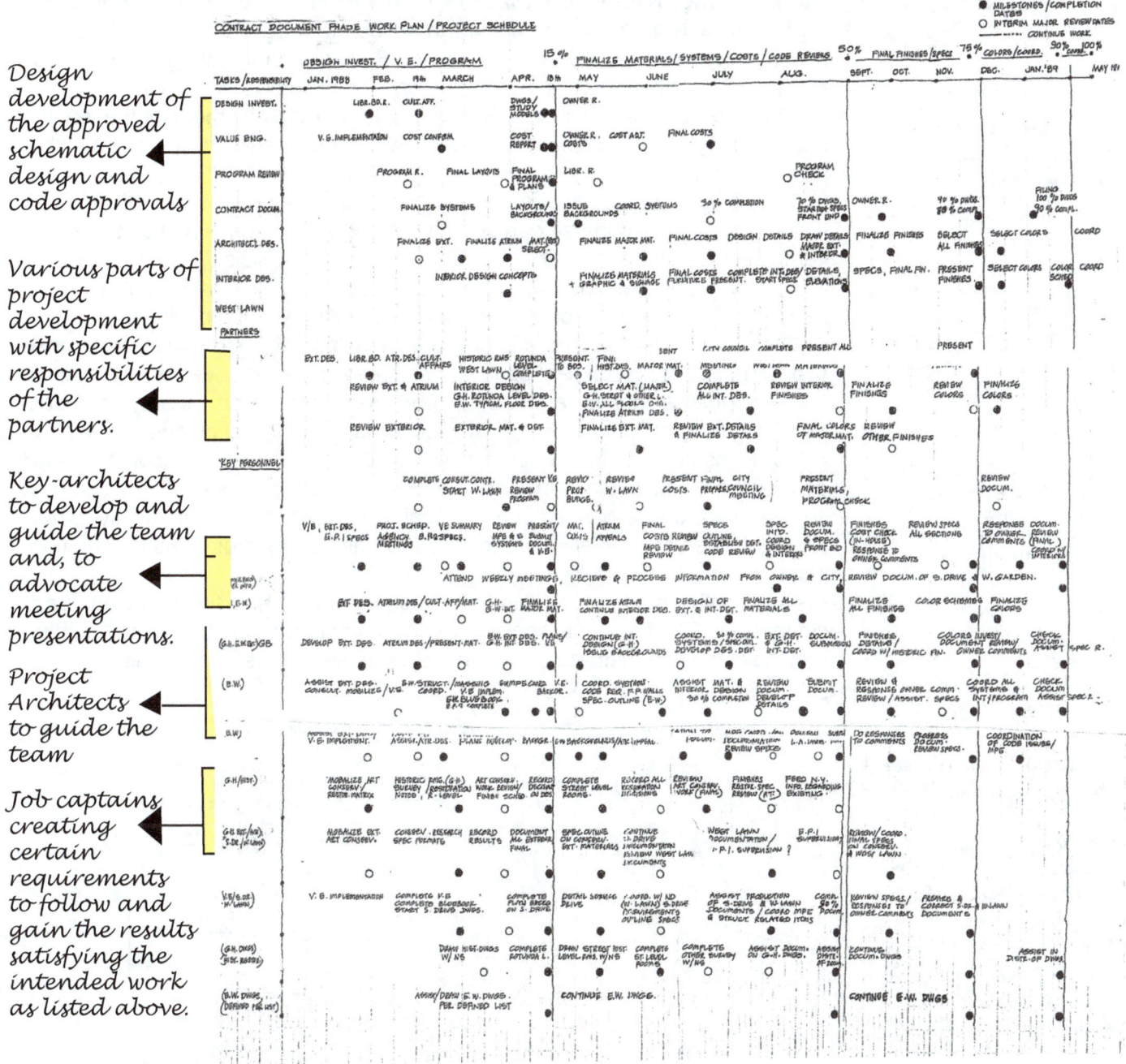

Design development of the approved schematic design and code approvals

Various parts of project development with specific responsibilities of the partners.

Key-architects to develop and guide the team and, to advocate meeting presentations.

Project Architects to guide the team

Job captains creating certain requirements to follow and gain the results satisfying the intended work as listed above.

PROJECT SCHEDULE
Specifically, handling a massive project and working with partners and many team members, it is very active to create a project schedule which could include and organize, preparations of the Clients' meetings and required presentations of the documents. And later, other successful versions of project submissions, beginning with contractors positive-working on the project involvement and all city agencies' approvals, should be included.

Schematic design

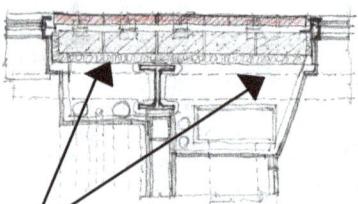

Exterior wall dimensions with critical impact and positive results

Exterior wall with extra width-dimensions & added acoustical quality: Vertical ductwork, electrical and plumbing supply units.

The railroad impacs the acoustical quality inside the school classrooms.

Underground water -holding area.

Such wall design and construction resolves the acoustical status of the classrooms by creating double-wall development to include conventional-ductwork, plumbing and vertical electrical units to serve all floors. The windows could have 3-glass layers to satisfy the required R-value.

8. EXTERIOR DESIGN
Exterior design: Wall details and construction approach

Before beginning work on the exterior design features, systems appearance, and intentions, **the architect can ideally spend a few days to initiate, appreciate, and approach a particular direction in developing exterior designs** and possibly achieving award-winning results. By following the suggested process and the steps mentioned as below, one can reach such design factors:

• **The exterior design can advocate a critical establishment** of the leading sustainability of the building related to the surrounding area, buildings and other pragmatic units.

• Plan diagrams should take into the consideration the locations of views as well as the sides of mid-rise or high-rise buildings. Planning of particular service items such as HVAC, plumbing, electrical and technological issues, elevators and exit stair area, and possibly primary structural and supporting walls will be a part of the determination of the type of wall construction and designs.

• Along with **the factors discussed regarding the acoustical resistance problem**, an architect can consider having a thick wall design to achieve better acoustical quality and stop sound disturbance from nearby railroads, manufacturing buildings, or similar disturbing building conditions. In addition to usual insulations, these same thick walls could act as an acoustical wall construction and could surround the vertical ductwork, electrical, plumbing supply units, and electrical/technological items that can run vertically, which will then divert horizontally to reach the program rooms around as per the floor plans.

Also the ceiling materials should provide sound absorption, fire safety and easy cleanability. Otherwise, the spoken words may not be understood, and teachers may have to raise their voices leading to increased stress and fatigue.

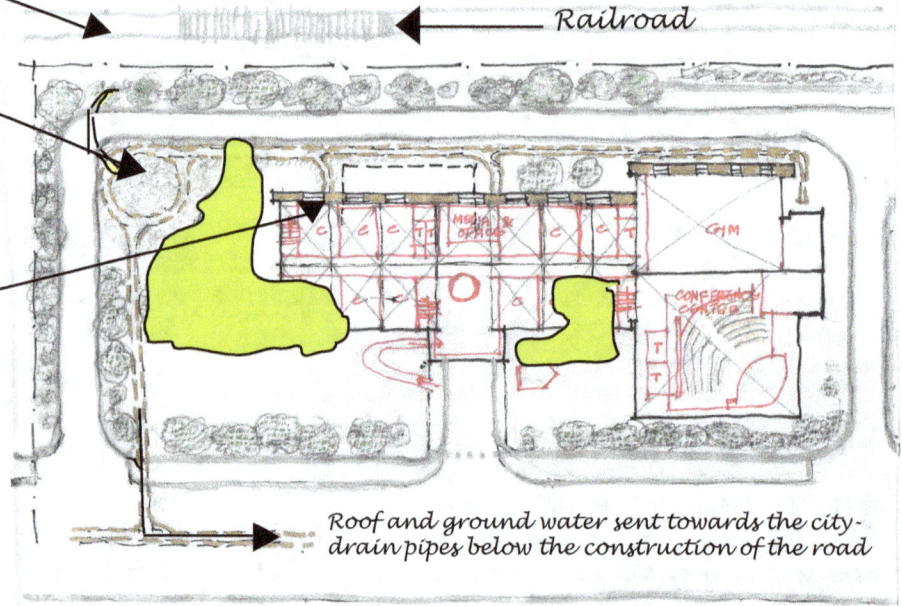

A High School - First floor plan with back wall aspect.

Schematic design

It is intentional to provide the top canopies and extended side units to control and arrange the sun shading coefficient and thermal performance of the glass units.

A high-rise building elevation with different window sizes could be planned: The windows could be designed with variable dimensions and at locations as per the floor plans and interior spaces if the structural columns are inside the exterior walls.

- **The exterior window design of high-rise residential or office buildings could vary from floor to floor** because the same units may not be entirely aligned above one another or the office-spaces may be designed for different users from floor to floor. In such exposition, the exterior design of the walls and entire project could be challenged to the variable floor-to-floor solutions. Also, the same surfaces could be designed with varied shapes and forms as selected with particular design efforts.

The architect will decide whether it is necessary to match or control the external material used in the project with the surrounding buildings. The decision may sometimes depend on the voice of the surrounding community. As far as the style or type of exterior surface design is to be created and selected, it might not be necessary to match, control, or reverse the design compared to the adjacent building surfaces. For example, depending on the surrounding, variable community spirits, the architect would finalize such decisions; to use brick, stone, concrete, metal panels, plaster, or other materials.

- The exterior design process can create a critical establishment of the leading sustainability of the building related to surrounding area, buildings, and logical units. The choice of exterior material for a renovation project will depend in part on, whether it is possible to repair or rebuild existing surfaces. However, existing historic building should be handled to succeed the original favorable inviting features. Besides, the replacement of materials should be appropriately checked with mock-ups.

As mentioned before, **exterior brick wall mock-ups** can be used to finalize its construction approval.

It is essential to check the contractors' work by specifying and checking sample-mock-ups of the major products in the projects to enhance the final and proper construction status of the buildings.

49

Schematic design

Working models

RESIDENTIAL HOUSE TYPE 1

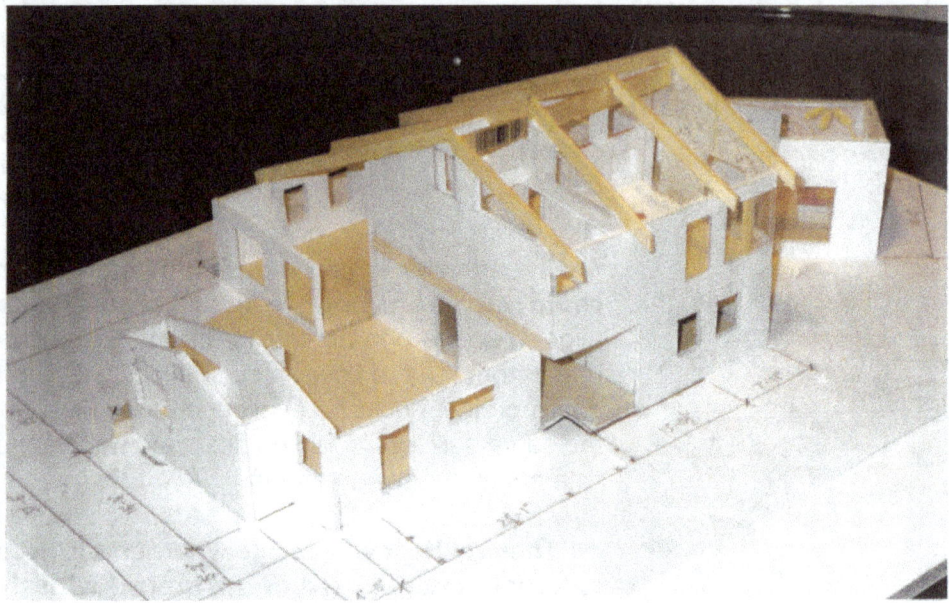

The skylights in the living room were selected towards Northside to achieve minimum sunshine but the direct lighting in the room in addition to the windows

After producing this model, the client was very idealistic regarding proceeding with the renovation and upper floor addition.

9. WORKING MODEL:

After completing the primary design process, **it is a good idea and proper time to prepare a working model** using typical and straightforward materials such as cardboard.

Sometimes such model may not be a final version indicating the final schematic design. However, the model can be assumed as an advanced phase of backup to 3-D creation because it supports the realistic imagination and serves the purpose of enhancing the thinking process for actual design elements. **It also initiates the architect to make his or her vision and intention clear** while pursuing exterior and interior design, thereby demonstrating a design expertise. It is also a lot easier to move forward with the plan proceeding with specific shapes, forms, colors, textures, light reflections or shades when the architect's mind has an actual view set-up in the model form of the building project. When seen in the model—such process forwards the imagination of the final vision of exterior design, interior areas, and material selections.

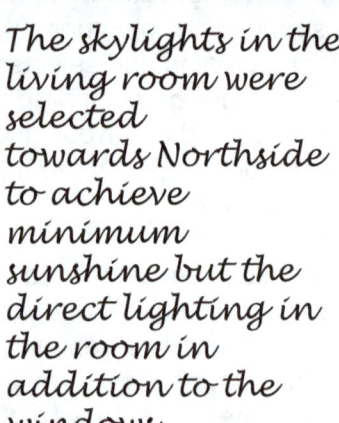

Working Model - (built at Misra & Associates) Marcy Houses Entrance: See pages 32 and 33. It was created to help the final design details and shapes to formalize the ADA ramp areas and the seating version with steps.

The ability to see the project in the model form further clarifies the 3-D view of the building project at the same locations and actual space impacts, and helps the architect to imagine the final design and details of all areas, materials, and shapes.

Models are also useful in reviewing the impact of outside sunshine and solving the impact of sun, shade, and wind aspects by possibly adding the shadow patterns and shapes.

Schematic design

New Residential House-Type 2

Working models

House Model with surrounding views such as bay area and surrounding site area.

B - Bedroom
BA - Bathroom
D - Den
DK - Deck
DR - Dining Room
E - Entrance
K - Kitchen
L - Living Room
LA - Laundry Room
LR - Library
P - Pantry
S - Stairs

First floor plan - model *Second floor plan - model*

As a summary, with the support of presenting working models with even unfinished schematic design (but showing the floor plans and adjacent site issues), the client will understand the architect's approach to gain approval of the planning arrangements.

BIM and Revit create 3-Ds and moving images, showing specific selected materials, shapes, and forms. Also, as mentioned above, **the models help further to manage possible choices, impressions, and feelings to design and decide impressive material selections, shapes, and forms.**

These working models should show planned areas on every floor and some innovation and direction of exterior design such as solid walls, prefabricated unit walls, locations of windows, openings, and setbacks of the upper floors. Also, such models envision the proposed curtain wall locations, entrance locations, canopies, and sill projections in general format for various types of professional buildings. **Beyond this version, these models help contractors to advance their understanding of the designed building and some preconception of the proposed details.**

Working models and even unfinished schematic design (but showing the floor plans and adjacent site issues), will help the client understand **the architect's approach to planning and conveying the style of users.**

Schematic design

RESIDENTIAL HOUSE PROJECT WITH WORKING MODEL.

Some clients cannot visualize the project details related to room locations, sizes, and impacts of circulation. "When one of my clients had difficulty in understanding the plan layouts, a relative in their team had to walk around and explain how all adjacent rooms were approached; turn right, turn left, continue walking to reach a particular place." In response to this problem, I then prepared a working model, and it was helpful in going forward and acquiring the client's approval of the plans and design for building the house with a major renovation

When the client is facing an impact of a particular unexpected state of the unfinished project, a working model is required to continue with their understanding of the new and revised plans.

Presenting working models along with the incomplete schematic design (which would include the floor plans and adjacent site issue) **will help the client understand the architects' approach towards resolving the planning arrangements as well as the intent of interior design** (room locations, shapes, forms and materials selections). Such process helps to go forward toward acquiring the client's approval of the schematic design and plan layouts.

Also, I have experienced that working models, as well as the finalized design models, help contractors to understand the process and the intention of the building details rapidly. One of the contractors used the working models throughout the construction phase of the house. It is particularly useful if building working model is a part of the design process and goes hand in hand with its following aspects such as the contractors' work as shown on page 53.

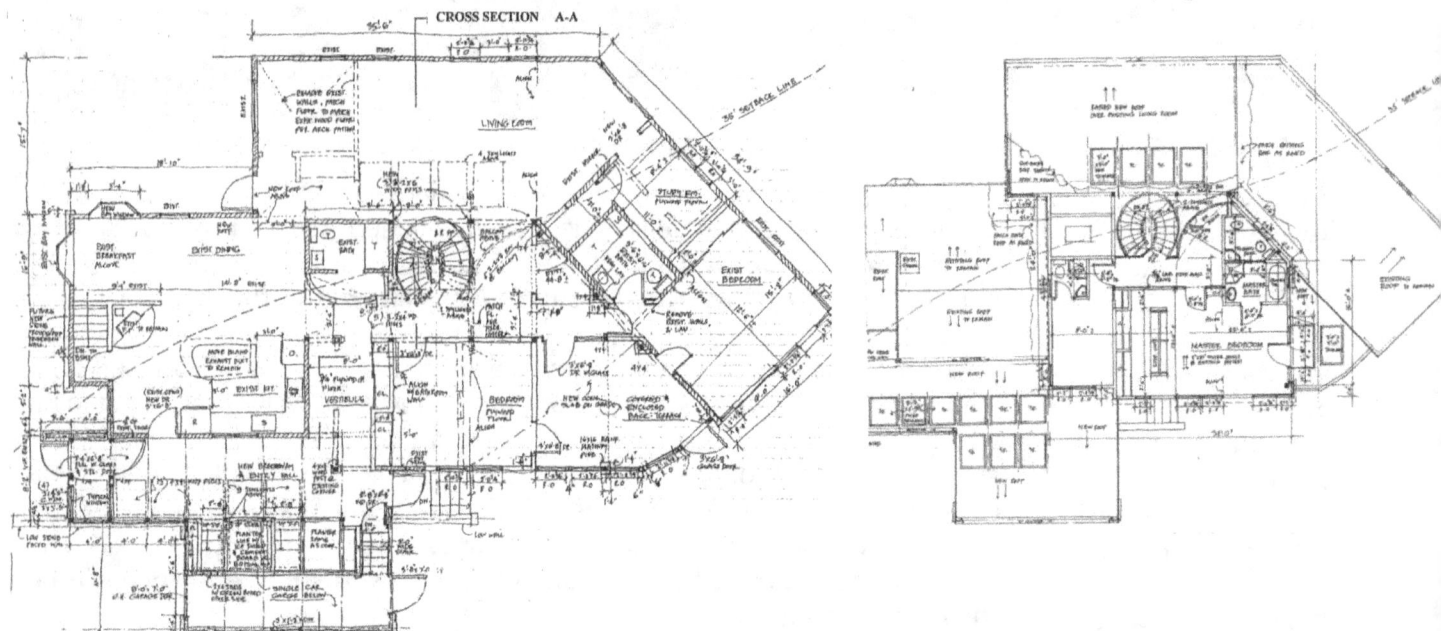

First Floor Plan
With entrance lobbies, kitchen, dining room, living room and one bedroom

Second Floor Plan
With oval stair, corridors with Museum like paintings, master bedroom and another bedroom

Schematic design

Residential House Type 1

Residential House models

Additionally, I have experienced that **the clients use the built working models that help them see shapes, sizes, circulation** because they may not be able to understand the layout and design of spaces just by viewing the 3-D/BIM images. Models also serve much the same function for the architect, sparking imagination and making it easier and faster to achieve design goals.

Current technology presents many 3-D and BIM settings in general, with the vision and understanding of the plans. **Also, the clients necessarily need the complete knowledge of the spaces, circulation, size, and shapes of the rooms, units, or how to access those areas.** Some clients may not necessarily understand and visualize the actual forms, the imagination of final views of walls, ceilings, and windows, just by looking at drawings and even pictures.

When the architects create models, **the clients advance their review and imagination** to think about the shapes, relative surfaces, and locations of the walls, windows, floors, and ceilings in actual working model formats. **It is also easier and faster for the architects to imagine, design, and achieve design goals** that they initiate and finalize both the exterior and interior design looking at models by approaching the shapes, relative surfaces and locations of the walls and windows.

Contractor built the house quickly by using the models throughout their construction process, by professionally thinking about the related details.

Contractor's work *Model*

Model *Model*

Schematic design

HIGH-RISE BUILDING ENTRANCE LOBBY, STAIR, AND EXIT DOORS

ENTRANCE LOBBY: ALSO PLANNED AS AN EXIT LOBBY

Hi-rise Tower Plan Shows with two apartment plans which were able to be combined as one Condo-Apartment.

As an exit lobby it is required to close the doors and space next to the elevators when all users have left and are away from the elevators.

Exit Stair: Exiting direction through the lobby.

Note: All lobby walls need to be 1 1/2 hr. fire rated as exiting requirements. All finishes should also be fire-resistant material quality

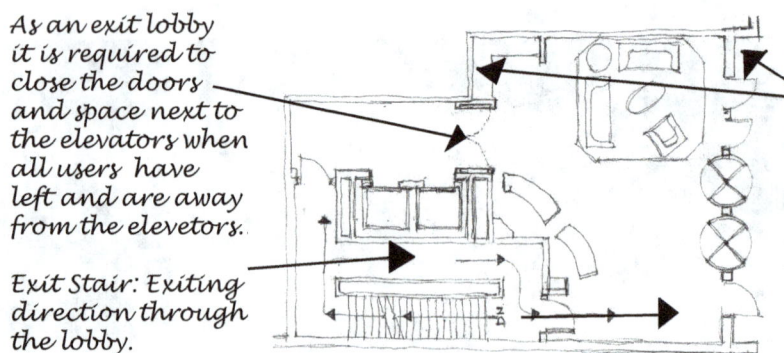

HI-RISE RESIDENTIAL BUILDING:

Sometimes, **a client for a high-rise condominium building may have difficulty understanding the plan drawings and may not notice that the upper-level units will not meet the marketing criteria as large penthouses.** Unfortunately, if the architect would not know about this requirement, the selling aspect would not be determined well. As a result, the project needs to be rounded off with the expected huge apartments, especially at penthouse floor levels.

Fortunately, **the architect could plan and use the original apartment layouts to just remove a small portion of the separating wall between the two condo-penthouses** and add a couple of doors, and only changing also a couple of room layouts to obtain the revised location of an additional bedroom and related bathroom. By enlarging the total area as one penthouse unit by connecting two condos and providing it twice as large as expected, the marketing aspects would be resolved of the built building without any problems in planning, estimates, or final marketing issues.

B - Bedroom
BA - Bathroom
D - Dining area
DR - Dining Room
E - Entrance
K - Kitchen
L - Living Room
LR - Library
MB - Master Bedroom
P - Powder Rooms

To combine the two Condo-Apartments, a closet and the divider wall portion could be removed, and a kitchen could be redesigned and built as a Master Bathroom

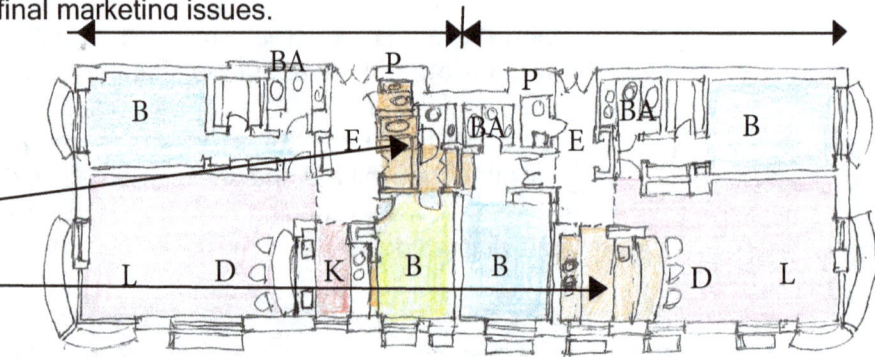

Two Original Condo-Apartments - Layout

As a result, the main entrance lobby area could be enlarged and connected to access the bedrooms. Also, the previous kitchen area could be arranged as a bathroom; a part of the Master Bedroom. The new Dining Room is connected to the Kitchen

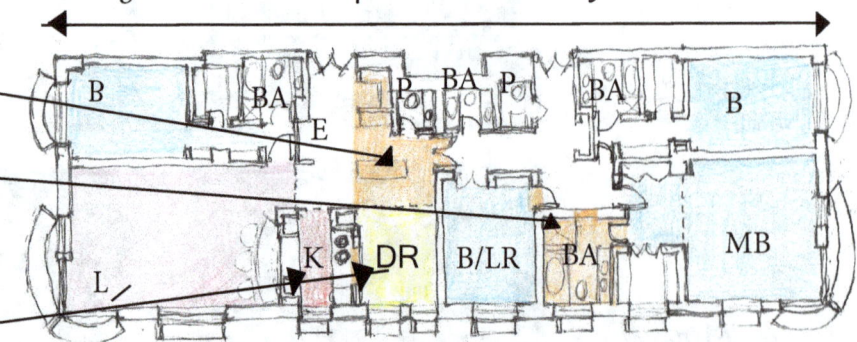

Turned into One Condo-Apartment with minimum Changes

Schematic design

10. CLIENT REACTIONS AND BUILDING SYSTEMS

Building systems should be verified and initiated as conducting its accuracy related to the primary program and design intentions. Therefore, the architect should contact the client and discuss fundamental requirements in detail and proper relationship with the direction of the schematic layout. It should include:
- Structural, mechanical, electrical, geotechnical, environmental, theatrical, demolitions and detailed version of kitchen, elevators, cafeteria and other unique locations used by the attendees.

With the support of presenting working models and even unfinished schematic design (but showing the floor plans and adjacent site issues), the client will understand the architect's approach to gain approval of the planning arrangements.

11. BUDGET ESTIMATES:

During the design process, architects should achieve project estimates so that the clients have reasonable and acceptable information helping their status for affording and going forward with the building project. All clients, city agencies, developers, individual project clients, healthcare professionals need to see shapes, sizes, circulation, and all building owners need to know the estimates at each phase.

- The architect can find the costs of the various major components of a project by contacting the manufacturers; for example, the price of a curtain wall will vary according to the type of design details, glass layers and sizes, and acoustic quality assurance. Therefore, an average cost estimate may not be sufficient if it does not include the architect's particular design style such as requirements of the curtain wall and its attachments to the building structure or walls.

- It is a good idea **to confirm the quality selections of the systems estimated by cost consultant.** Such efforts will move the project forward in a positive direction and help the client understand the details of various stages of development.

SPECIFICATIONS:

During the schematic design process, the architect should find out details of possibly suggested and selected materials, and they should quickly review the necessary specifications of those elements. A similar process should go forward regarding installations of superior materials. **Even though the schematic design phase may not include all detail items, the team should find and record the practical information in the file** with following the service of specifications and detail standards related to the items.

Such efforts will support and forward the project development in more positive directions. This process would make it convenient for the clients as well to understand clarified details about various stages of the project development.

Design Development Phase

Design Development Phase

The purpose of the design development phase is to completely process and be ready to create construction documents including working drawings, specifications, cost estimates and the intention of the site supervision.

Usually, the design development expands the schematic design with a realistic approach to the construction process and determination to fix the place and to meet the issues of the program, visibility in the city, town and possibly it would lead towards the status of the award-winning project.

Therefore, design development is an essential working process, to advance the reality of the schematic design, to achieve the final approval from the clients, the future contracts with contractors and subcontractors and, to establish the estimate practically correct. With such process, there is no surprise regarding the final estimates are close to the bidding results by the contractors.

Design Development Phase

Contents:

SCOPE OF WORK

SPACE PLANNING

EXTERIOR WALL DESIGN AND DETAILS

DESIGN DEVELOPMENT SUPPORTED BY WORKING MODELS

BUDGET ORGANIZATION AND BUILDING MATERIAL SELECTIONS

CONSTRUCTION PROCESS, INTERIOR DESIGN, AND MATERIAL SELECTIONS

WINDOWS, CURTAIN WALLS, AND DOORS- SELECTIONS

STAIRS

SPECIFICATIONS

Design Development Phase

Possible diagrams about DD Dimensions

Residential House Type 1

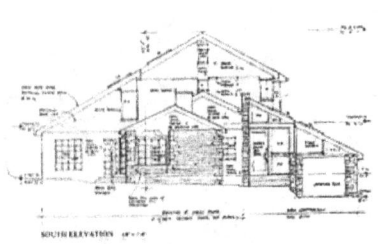
Front Elevation

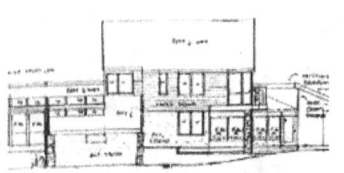
Southside elevation

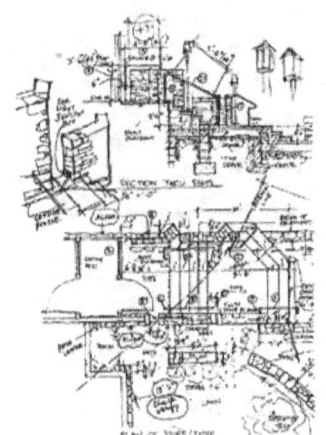
Entrance stair Detail

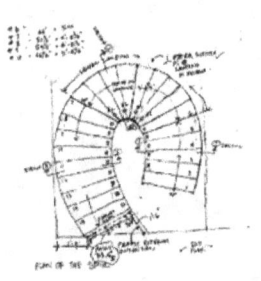
Oval Interior stair

Second floor plan

Primary 2nd floor plan, section, and elevation was developed to advance the schematic design.
And the entrance design with high-end attractive invitation was detailed during Design Development.

DESIGN DEVELOPMENT PHASE:

With the project moving forward in a positive direction because of a favorable schematic design phase and earlier client meetings, it is time to start organizing the teams responsible for the remaining aspects of the project to advocate further provisions of the successful work process. **It should forward the architectural, interior, visual and positive construction impacts, and, structural, mechanical, electrical, geographical, curtain wall consultant, landscaping, and technological requirements.**

Since the design development phase is about a two-to-three-month period, the architects/staff have to create, check, follow-up, and almost finalize the following and other included items. This description will lead the teams to emphasize their **scope of work during design development to organize and complete the next construction document phase in order.**

SCOPE OF WORK: PLANNING ASPECTS

1. It is essential *to confirm the planning issues and proceed with the plan dimensions* to include most construction dimensions of the thickness of walls, floors, ceilings, and even doors, and all mechanical, plumbing, electrical, and media unit spaces. Thus, **the expected and actual program areas are saved and are available within the gross building area as final results during the construction process**. In this work process, one needs to consider the following ideas:

- Structural support, acoustic requirements, finishes of the interior wall surfaces, floors, and ceilings that need to be designed and included in walls, floors and ceiling thickness dimensions.
- *Spaces required by the HVAC and Electrical systems and, technological equipment* need to be added in addition to the actual space program required areas. **This process is governed by coordination meetings with consultants** even though their work may not be complete until the end of the design development phase. The project architects need to include specific known dimensions for the above units while further developing the plans and documents. Otherwise, the final project will not be able to succeed in maintaining the program requirements.

Design Development Phase

SPACE PLANNING

- *Such planning version depends on site and soil conditions,* (such as water table, roots, clay, sand. and specific soil locations). The ground floor, basement levels, and foundation type planning will be created based on the results of those issues. Therefore, ideally, **a geotechnical consultant should be hired.**

- *While adjusting and finalizing, dimensions for the plans,* the architects need to consider the actual realistic results of the construction process. As we continue horizontally and vertically to stabilize the sizes, **it is helpful to add 1 inch or so extra dimensions within each 10-foot unit-dimension.** So that the final construction results on the site will still adjust and provide the required program spaces, exit width dimensions, workability of door swing results, ADA and code dimensions and railing dimensions (projections). Similar details will otherwise further appear with problems in the next documentation phase and during construction work process.

1. *Working models:* These models also help contractors to review drawings to see details of their forthcoming work. As mentioned in the schematic design phase, working models help clients visualize and understand the space and make informed decisions about the details, reviewed by them. Besides, they could go forward and advocate initial decisions, circumstances and interpret the results of the built building.

2. The architects and consultants should coordinate *structural design and dimensions during design development.* To proceed with the completion of the floor plans, the architects need to consider sufficient aspects of the structural support systems with attachments. It includes finish materials with its supporting studs, metals, hangers, electrical tubing, fire-protection-insulation, wiring, as well as other HVAC vertical ducts, plumbing pipes and other space-occupying materials such as duct hangers, ceiling attachments, and supports. **When these efforts are neglected, we face problems with other items with their dimensions such as below the ceilings, within the rooms and open spaces.**

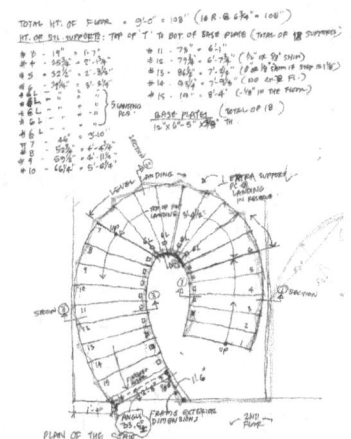

Stair design during the Design Development was determined with the 'step-rise' dimesions, shapes and structursl supports under the steps as shown on page no. 64.

Similar aspects are also related to *achieving ceiling heights.* At most locations, the architects need to consider the dimensions required for horizontal ducts, with their crossing impact and hangers; a continuation of the plumbing pipes with its required slopes; and layouts of the main electrical cables and technological unit connections. Besides, the possible acceptable deflections of structural steel units do influence the results of final ceiling heights. Therefore, **ideally, the required dimensions of the ceiling space should include two extra inches of space to determine and achieve the ultimate space design.**

In most cases, these details may be manipulated in construction documents, but by adding a few inches, they become a proper part of selected dimensions established in this phase **and eventually lead to accurate construction documents and building construction status.**

Design Development Phase

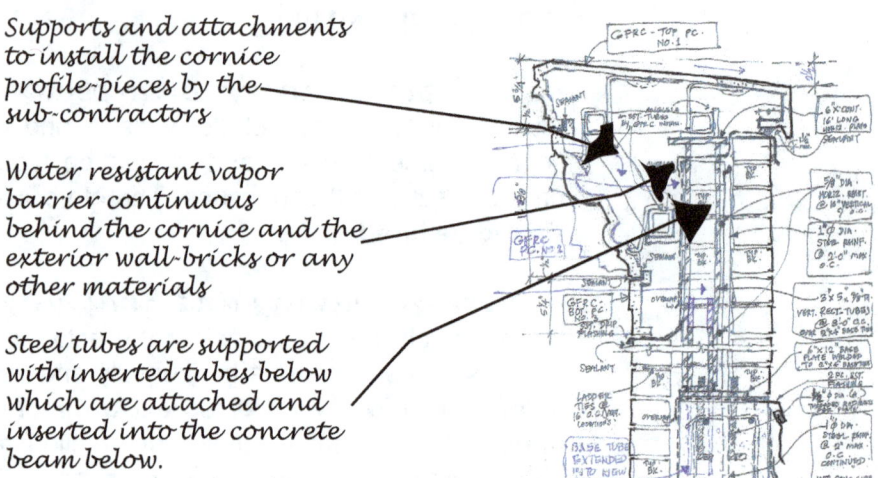

Supports and attachments to install the cornice profile-pieces by the sub-contractors

Water resistant vapor barrier continuous behind the cornice and the exterior wall-bricks or any other materials

Steel tubes are supported with inserted tubes below which are attached and inserted into the concrete beam below.

Exterior parapet wall with materials design, selections and structural attachments/supports

EXTERIOR WALL DESIGN AND DETAILS

3. *Exterior-wall thickness dimensions:*
It should include the exterior surface material with finishes, attachments and structural supports, grids, insulation-material thickness, wall supports, and interior finish materials. **While confirming the overall wall thickness, architects need to consider exterior planning and dimension requirements for items** such as electrical outlets, wiring cables, heating transmission, and plumbing pipes if planned. Also, the architects should determine the necessary dimensions with the structural engineers to configure the design to withstand wind loads, speeds, impacts with related connections, and the ground conditions, foundations including seismic implications.

4. *Materials design and selections*
Formatting such process with its details is necessary during this phase. **It is essential to find and confirm whether:**
• The materials are available.
• Suppliers and installers have the attachments for installing the materials.
• The architect has reviewed final design decisions with the client and obtained approval. Sample mock-ups are helpful in moving the process along.

5. *Mechanical and electrical system collaborations.*
Even though the consultants may not be able to complete their final design development status quickly, **architects should find and assume enough spaces within the plans and ceiling spaces** as mentioned before when working during the schematic design phase. BIM and Revit may subordinate the information, but finally, not all dimensions for hangers and supports and cable sizes may be reflected on those drawings. If not, such difficulties could ultimately raise sizes with problems during the construction process and create change orders. Therefore, it is essential to consider such details during design development and later on, a part of the final construction documents.

Design Development Phase

New Residential House-Type 2

DESIGN DEVELOPMENT SUPPORTED WITH WORKING MODELS

6. *Working model.* The model helps focus **the impact of the architect's progressive thinking on design goals, material decisions, and actual resulting installations** as well as the client's understanding of the project design development. All of these will contribute to the successful completion of the design development documents. One should decide to do the model using the 1/2" = 1' scale.
Models are usually built at a scale of ¼" = 1' if they are 100' long or larger dimensions.

Exterior and Interior model- Shows primary entrance (Entry stairs are shown on the floor plans on page 43)

The model should be built using at least ½" =1' or even 1" =1' scale to determine the final best results of a front entry area and the design of significant portions of the building. **Such range also makes it possible to think about planning and to check a part of the exterior or interior wall patterns and, final selections quickly indicating the satisfactory results.** It includes visible patterns, details, expansion joint locations, details of the parapets, window sills, jamb trims, headers trims, canopies, entrance canopies, base details as well as corner details. And masonry patterns, vertical expansion-joint patterns as per planned structural details or for vertical masonry details (for most projects) are to be included.

BUDGET ORGANIZATION AND BUILDING MATERIAL SELECTIONS

7. *Budget estimates.* The cost consultants could start their work by adding information about the specific primary materials and systems such as curtain walls, acoustic material selections, lighting selections (including selected outlets), exhaust grille designs, and overall cost status of all items to be finalized by the consultants.

8. *Interior design layout and materials.* During schematic design and design development process, **the architects need to begin thinking about the size and layout of the interior furniture shelving, working tables and planned exit dimensions** of the exit aisles in large rooms, such as theaters, meeting rooms, seating areas and corridor-type separations between unit spaces. **These efforts then provide the basis for the successful planning of the building and also define the intentions of interior design** related to shapes, forms, and impacts of the exterior walls, finished floors and ceilings a number practically and fruitfully. The depth and thickness of the finished floor material will vary with some cables, its locations, and other considerations because of the current status of the computers and media equipment.

Design Development Phase

CONSTRUCTION PROCESS SELECTIONS, INTERIOR DESIGN AND MATERIAL SELECTIONS

9. *Ideally, interior designers should also be involved from the beginning of an architectural design process.* During design development, **the architects should resolve and collaborate on strong floor support, provisions for electrical and cable systems in floor slabs, and floor finishes** or those above the structural slab. Delaying such decisions could create cost changes, ceiling height issues, and electrical unit details and layouts. As currently, there have been various systems of such provisions to access powers and networks, therefore finishes shall be revealed as per construction design process. It is also possible that changes occur later as required by the professional business users in many office buildings, stores, workshops, and similar business unit projects.

• *Similar to architectural practice, the interior design, materials, and estimates need to be continually monitored for availability.* **The interior designer and the architect also consider the design intent, the psychological impact on the interior spaces,** paint decisions and, the weight, size, construction, and finishes of furniture such as leather, fabrics, wood, steel, copper, plastic, glass and other materials.

Some limited multi-story luxury condominium buildings may be planned using Fire Retardant Wood in the exterior bearing walls and studs but allowed by IBC permits and possibly using NFPA 13 fire sprinkler system.

• Window blinds and drapes and, the quality of the glass used in windows and doors shall be designed and approved by the client. These items help control the impact of sun and shade patterns on the space and its usability.

• **Since the time required installing the interior objects/items may be much shorter than that needed for the manufacturing process**, sometimes it may be necessary to order those materials before completion of the interior design and finishing of spaces on the site.

Completion of the interior and exterior with the finish materials must be coordinated with *the installation of planned construction materials.*

Examples:
      1. Selecting granite from and at the quarry location,
      2. Approving oxidized bronze over lacquered bronze and
      3. Judging the value of colors in mixing of pigments with the clear base
.... for infilling the existing marble veins to match existing floor finish.

• *Nearly all spaces will require electrical connections, outlets, and network connections. Therefore, the final architectural and interior design efforts need to assess and include all such requirements.* Otherwise, final interior designs end up with hanging cables or on top of floor surfaces, which is not a prudent, successful design version. This planning benefits the completion of the working drawings and, later, the construction process.

• Specifically, the theater stage, gymnasium stage-area, meeting rooms, conference rooms, office rooms, kitchens, dining rooms, media rooms and waiting rooms need such electrical and technical service requirements, which may not necessarily be used every day but are required. Such provisions should be established and made possible for consultants to organize their drawings and contractors to install if necessary in an earlier contract phase.

Design Development Phase

Interior Gypsum Board Walls:

Even though there are standards and typical wall sections, available as diagrams and drawing pages in the firms, it is important to study, make decisions and confirm room locations, to decide the necessary fire-rating, acoustical and wall finishes as well as construction status requirements. For example, some gypsum board walls are to be additionally reinforced types or to resolve the wetness aspects.

It is intentional to provide the top canopies and side extended shadow units to control and arrange the sun-control.

The canopies should not hold rainwater or snow/ice.

Interior Gypsum Board Walls:

Each side of the walls should support the interior space requirements such as; acoustics, wetness resistance and some structural support for shelves etc.

WINDOWS, CURTAIN WALLS AND DOORS

10. *Windows, doors, and other access-or-unit doors.* As a successful design, the following items are part of the total, highly admired exterior design:

a. *Windows*
• Many cities have codes that regulate the total window areas related to the percentage of the exterior wall area of a high-rise residential building. This regulation is often associated with energy code issues.
• **Mostly the architect needs to start with the design aspects of user expectations, basic daylight version for energy usage, accelerating views, and sometimes ventilation issues,** particularly for residential buildings.
• The architect must also check the acoustical ratings for window units. Projects located next to railroad tracks, highways, manufacturing facilities, and other busy areas may require three-layer glass windows to gain a minimum forty-four R-value or a Low-e status. In such cases, one may need to think of the planning of the program spaces facing each side of the buildings. At the same time, realistic, proper planning to respond it correctly in such site location is also necessary.
• **Acoustics are of particular importance to consider** in conference rooms, teaching classrooms, theaters, concert halls, and most offices in the business or public buildings as well as bedroom areas in the residential buildings.

b. *Curtainwalls*
• As part of the specifications, architects should consider and provide specific statements regarding the actual manufacturing of the curtain walls. In general, related to the built building with structural slabs and other structural elements, the actual timely dimensions; **heights and widths of the planned curtain walls should be verified on site before its production, to organize the final installation.**

Hi-rise building structure and the curtainwall attachments.

Design Development Phase

Interior Design-Railing Details created during the design development phase. (In my previous house)

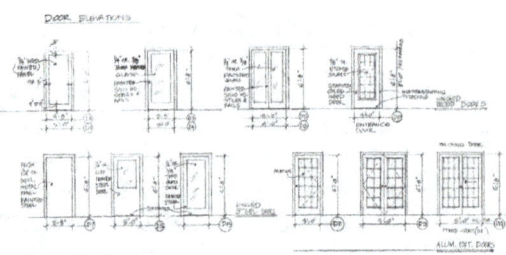

DOOR DESIGN & ELEVATIONS

The right side tall wall has painting color-strips to invite you to go upstairs!

c. Doors
- Exterior doors require the accessibility systems, smooth operation, and security aspects to be determined while selecting its manufacturers during the design process.
- Interior doors need attention to the design elements (materials, views to all across the interior room spaces with glass panels), fire ratings, and security controls.
- Overall headers, door jambs, and bottom sills with proper detailing are essential items. At all exterior-facing locations, the waterproofing layers need to continue outward and down to forward the water outside in continuous directions.

d. Access Doors
Access doors are particularly crucial for electrical, exhaust, and fire protection.

Upstairs (In my previous house)

STAIRS
Since some stairs are used many times during days, **the design has to be an attractive, usable and inviting version for users beyond the current required code contents.**

Specifically, in residential houses, they need to be well used and encouraging the owners.

Stair in the Residential House Type - 1
It is designed to access the bedrooms on the second floor and then access the living room and dining room in a favorite mode to see the invited guests sitting downstairs in the living room.

The 12" and 16" long SST. tubes were connected to formulate the railings

Structural supports are seen from the second floor

SPECIFICATIONS:
During design development, all specification items need to be displayed and specified in the final specification document standards as mentioned above with the confirmation of the process of installation. Such actions need to be already confirmed and understood during this phase. **Architects should include the correct detail description and installation standards and statements.**

Design Development Phase

RESIDENTIAL HOUSE
TYPE 1

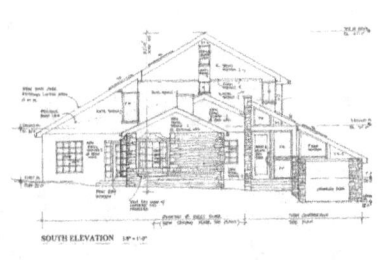

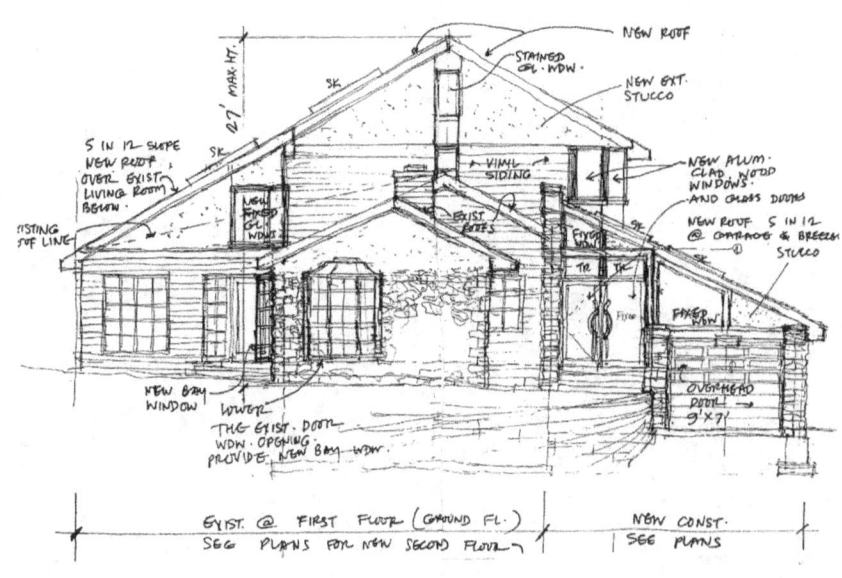

Initial preliminary design showing the results of suggested renovation / new inviting house aspects.

Final Elevation appreciated by the client after looking at the working model to agree with further detail of exterior elevations to go forward with the final construction documents

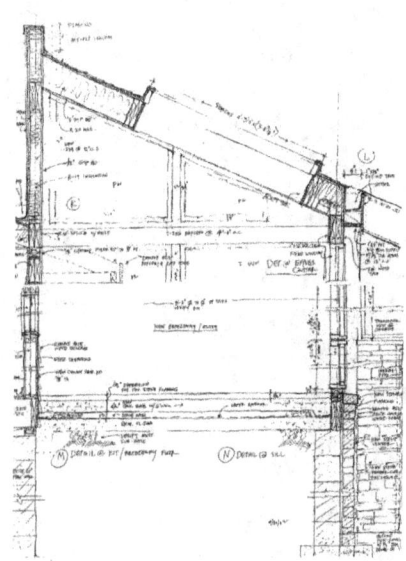

Entry Plan to the Entrance Lobby:

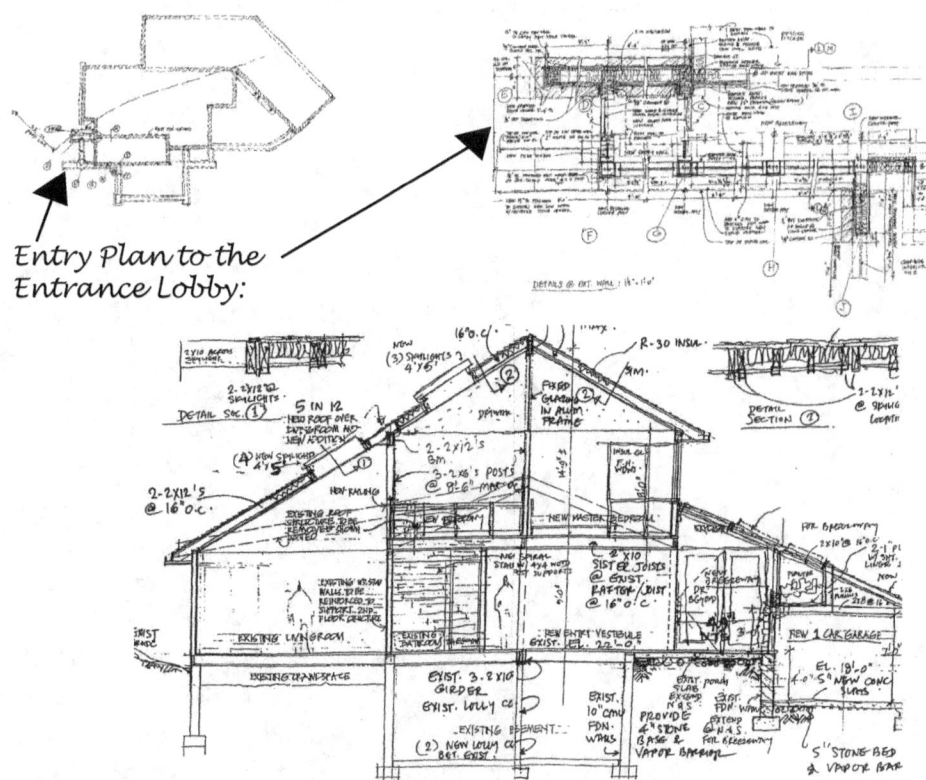

Section through the Entrance Lobby:

Going forward with the Part of construction documents

Status of construction in design development phase to confirm shapes, forms and materials

Interior Design Phase

Interior Design Phase

The interior design process is often not approached as a part of the early phases of a project. Thereby, it does not get started or created by the team in the first period in a progressive direction, and the actual process of the design of the building or rooms, on the same site, is affected to some extent.

However, colors and shapes, furniture design and spacing, impact and support the many aspects of the completion of the design, including the client's acceptance. It is required to proceed appropriately with the affluent documents. Interior design decisions related to space availability, configuration status and the visual impact of furniture affect the planning and the construction documents.

Therefore, an interior designer and the architect should start creating ideas and styles during the schematic design phase. And they should look ahead at how the plans will affect and reflect the entire success and quality of the building project. Some architects also pursue and act as interior designers.

Interior Design Phase

Contents:

INTERIOR DESIGN PROCESS

EMERGING PRESENTATION OF THE INTERIOR DESIGN FOR THE CLIENTS

PAINTING AND COLOR SELECTIONS

TWENTY-FIRST CENTURY ADVOCATING INTERIOR DESIGN PROCESS

INTERIOR DESIGN DOCUMENTS

BIDDING PROCESS AND CONTRACTS

Interior Design Phase

Residential House Type - 2

The interior planning of the House-Model, represents the related room spaces on the second floor: Bedrooms, Decks, Toilets & access stair; all rooms enhance the Bay views.

Working Model

INTERIOR DESIGN PROCESS

Interior designers and architects work together to create and finalize the material selections, design decisions, and availability of the equipment and installations. Before this technical aspect, it is prudent to start the process during the schematic design stage by following the intention of the original design process. **The working model guides and informs the primary process** because it shows the overall impact of planning decisions, a spatial review, and how the shapes of interior spaces support their usability.

EMERGING PRESENTATION OF THE INTERIOR DESIGN FOR THE CLIENTS

Managing client expectations and budgets is a critical part of this design phase. To gain buy-in from clients and learn about their vision for the interior spaces, historical basics, contemporary ideas, or past and present design versions, **it is helpful to the client and the architect to visit installations in some built-buildings**, existing buildings, perhaps including a range of styles and approaches. Such a practical approach will lead to approval of the design and support completion of the design development phase in a positive direction.

1. For example, a house with a small atrium or narrow light strip skylights engenders an attraction to pass through that area going towards the other expected rooms or units. A glass-block-atrium-like view is shown on the next page. Also, another house with skylights above the entrance lobby and the living room advances the life and daily life enthusiasms for the client as shown on page nos. 36 and 50.

Interior Design Phase

Residential House with Small Atrium

Residential House- With a Small atrium-like back entrance

Exterior and Interior Views

69

Interior Design Phase

Selection of the ceiling color
Selection of the wall color

House Interior- Dining Room- Selected colors are some indications of foods; carrot and green beans.

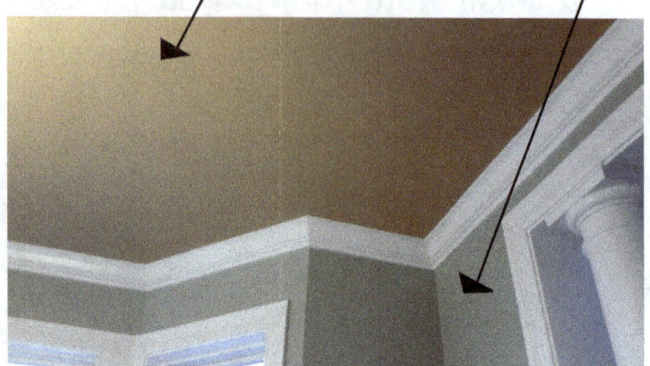

PAINTING AND COLOR SELECTIONS

2. *Decisions about paint, colors, and finishes should proceed after the architect's visual intentions and suggestions* and, when client expectations with decisions about finishes are settled. **It is helpful to hang color samples in the same area for at least a week or longer**, where they can be viewed during the day, evening, and at night. An architect can first get prepared, specific paint-color samples on eighteen-by-twety-four-inch-sized papers and keep them on the walls, ceilings or working unit cabinets as related to the painting locations. This process will show how light affects the colors as well as their view of emotional impact throughout the day and night; such efforts will help clients and architects to prompt their final approval and decisions about the paint selections.

On massive building projects, architects should insist on about 10′ x 10′ size sample models of the great paint samples in critical areas so that its approvals and other decisions can be finalized and advocated. This process should be designed, managed and included at the end of design development or at the beginning of working drawing documentation. Soothing colors, contrasting colors, and historical impacts are all imperative to gain results of any project style, design, and conditions.

Interior Design Phase

Original wall color on the wall was later tested with a new color sample for two weeks

Grey/greenish color sample left on the wall for two weeks

The interior design around the Kitchen had been uplifted with wall color and tile selection

Grey/greenish color selected for the wall

The interior design of the Kitchen had been uplifted with the tile selection to co-relate with the countertop granite color and the kitchen-cabinet unit finishes

Interior Design Phase

INTERIOR DESIGN PROCESS

TWENTY-FIRST CENTURY ADVOCATING INTERIOR DESIGN

3. *Interior design process varies among the types of projects.* Cultural activities buildings, educational unit schools, colleges and other versions, residential buildings with even more user processes, healthcare facilities, and business-related office buildings—all such projects will require special treatments, decisions, and budget control process to succeed with a final result of the fruitful and award-winning project completions. **The following items could be considered, resolved, and found during the interior design process:**

- *Since the twenty-first century is advocating some controlled spaces,* energetic technology forwarding the healthcare requirements, and comfortable as well as functionally designed furniture processes; **the solutions should be initiated early on with the assistance of the experienced staff or coordinators and partners**.

- *Hospitality and retail industries* may lead towards interior entertainment versions.

- *Healthcare and patients' living standards* will be related to new technologies forwarding the healthcare requirements and health-care or outpatient requirements. As an example, the interior version of the psychological/mental care hospitals needs to have very efficient and ideally pleasurable-looking versions to impact the patients' behaviors.

- *High-rise buildings will need flexible interior designs* because tenants or clients may change when they acquire their housing or business process design versions.

- *The business and working process inhibits work environments and surrounding amenities* as an interior and exterior design to deal with everyday aspects of their successful work. Open offices, conference and meeting rooms, private offices and lobbies are the specific versions of the interior design elements.

- *Advocating an Interior Design process while planning* a conference room, banquet hall, meeting boardroom, institute assembly hall, university lecture hall, a grand ballroom as a classroom or a meeting room and a hotel meeting room: All will require essential layouts, types of furniture turned into the client's intention with successful usage. Sometimes an interior design in Historic Renovation projects will be required to follow up with classic - interior design.

Interior Design Phase

BIDDING PROCESS AND CONTRACTS:

INTERIOR DESIGN DOCUMENTS

The selected materials, furniture and installation services should be reviewed to compose a proper, timely provision of the materials and furniture. Besides, the subcontractors or installation companies should be contacted to achieve the completion of all interior items to be supplied and installed before the opening days of the built project.

- **The following and some other unlimited items may be considered** during design development and should be ultimately agreed to and finalized when the construction or working documents are completed.

- Library book stacks.
- Reading room chairs, tables, and instruction stacks
- Public school furniture and science class equipment
- Theater seats, acoustical and theater- units and theater stage action units and furniture.
- Hospital equipment, electronic items, and healthcare-involved individual units
- Residential unit equipment; especially the kitchen supply and bathrooms.

The complete version shall be of all presentation items, media instruments, and types of equipment.

Construction Documents

Construction Documents

The construction document phase is a crucial step in the process leading to building construction. All of the documents should reinforce a realistic approach and to a complete installation working process on the site as well as the design intention by the architects, other consultants, and by the clients.

Then there will be fewer change orders and problems, which are unfortunately faced by the client and the architects. The time duration of installation is also important if all details, drawings, and specifications are issued correctly and on time.

(Of course, if the developers who create and stabilize the construction, then they may process and forward the contractors to work with the proper installation.)

Construction Documents

Contents:

STARTING CONSTRUCTION DOCUMENTS

MAJOR DOCUMENT SHEETS

SITE CONDITIONS

FLOOR PLANS

ROOF PLANS

BUILDING SECTIONS

EXTERIOR ELEVATIONS

CONSULTANTS' WORK STATUS

SPECIFICATIONS

CONSTRUCTION PROCESS VS. STANDARD CATEGORY

Construction Documents

Window schedules

Door schedules

STARTING WITH CONSTRUCTION DOCUMENTS

The architects should continue with the entire thinking process of construction phase while completing the construction documents.

If some timelines, impact of temperature during the construction process for the building and the surrounding site are not considered, **it could generate change orders** usually added by the contractors for a version of the extended time of completion. It is related to, for example, problems of mortar, grout, glass and glass block installations as well as sealants, waterproofing, etc.

Alternatively, the contractors need to manage on their own about the above issues and include within their approved bidding amount and, schedule of the building completion.

CONSTRUCTION DOCUMENTS

- *Construction document process begins immediately after the design development* phase because the whole team is aware of what would be going forward. This timeline is based on an assumption, that the architect has garnered the client's approval during the design development process and the project has been reviewed by the code approval agencies.

- **The utmost document sheets to start are:** Site plans, floor plans, roof plans, major cross sections of the building, leading interior wall sections, exterior elevations, ceiling plans, *door schedules,* headers, jamb and sill details, and hardware schedules, columns, *window schedules* as necessary. And further documents should include; window details, curtain wall details, parapet and rooftop detail sections with corner details, interior design, furniture schedule and any other specific requirement.

While completing these documents, the architects have to coordinate, check and forward the successful consultants' drawings and specifications. And throughout such process, the architects and consultants should input required efforts to deal with the site conditions.

- **Even though the architects may use typical details** for some of the above items to create the drawing sheets or use standards supplied by specific city agency-selected clients, *ideally, the architects should recheck further details.* It includes; schedules, and sketches to ensure their realistic adherence to the design intention, practical construction process, structural status to support each item, and overall waterproofing issues. **Otherwise, problems occur while the project proceeds with construction,** resulting in many RFCs, meetings, and schedule problems, all continuing until completion.

While changing the status of these technical details and manufacturers' suggested details, one should describe the recommendations and results to the clients. In essence, BIM and Revit category goes forward, but as previously mentioned, **the architect still should confirm and relate them to the initiated design intent and realistic approach toward construction details and, installation process** before finalizing these documents.

Construction Documents

MAJOR DOCUMENT SHEETS

- *While proceeding with the significant sheets noted earlier, the architect should always have meetings* with the structural, mechanical, electrical, geotechnical, theater, acoustic, security, and code consultants. Such process will help control expectations and ensure everyone is on the same page.

It will also enhance the consultants' final understanding and confirmation of their suggestions for the best systems, especially for green and energy-code aspects. Once apparently, the redesign and reinstallation of particular appliances in some tall buildings were required to resolve the problem. Therefore, rechecking of using such process of sustainability is necessary to establish the completion of the project.

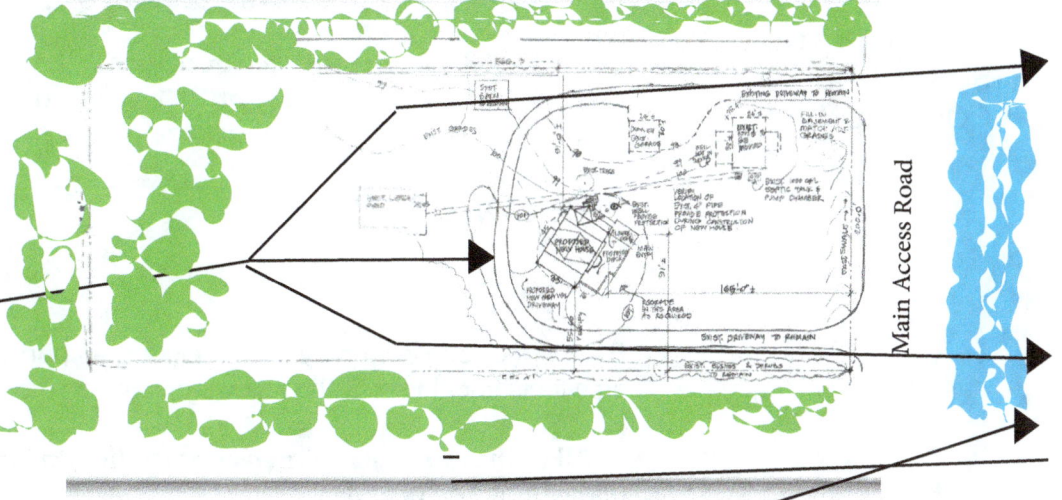

The house with the back side site location rounded with water drainage perforated pipes encircled with gravel layers in the ground and sloping towards the bay water direction delivering the water flow towards the bay side.

Site Plan - Soil and Groundwater condition.

The Water-Bay direction towards the front side of the site.

- **While proceeding with the in-house document preparations, architects need to visit and recheck the site property issues** (soil status and water-table levels, or storm influences) to go forward, capture and forecast possible determinations or updated design strategies and to coordinate with the community progress in the area. It may be necessary to add a proper supporting foundation; sloping ground-sites may require structural retaining walls and other adjustments in the size of pillars or piles. Sloping sites might also need underground perforated pipes around the project building with surrounding gravels to collect the flowing water on and below the ground away from the building and finally send it to the connected city drainage pipes. **It is one of the basics of eliminating the water-flow into basements or even flow around the perimeter of the building.**

- As one reaches about 50 percent of completion status, the architect should start the CD meetings with the estimators to finalize the accurate estimates.

Construction Documents

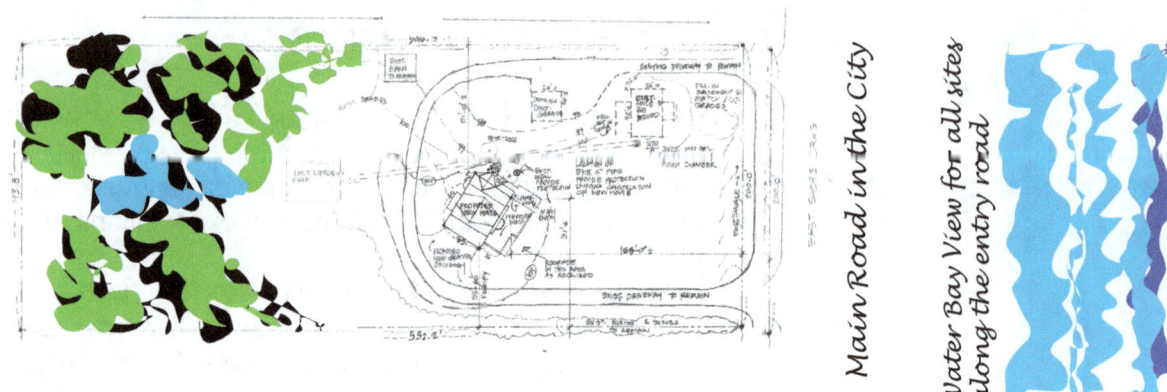

New Residential House-Type 2

SITE PLAN AND SURROUNDING CONDITIONS

Site Plan   Views from all rooms : See page 43 for floor plan and page 79 showing the model

2. In order to prepare documents in addition to its regular status, following relevant items could be considered by the teams to complete the work as final documentation.

SITE CONDITIONS

a. *Site Plans*

Even if the regular surveys are included as part of the overall documents, the architects should show the following items on the site plan:

- **All of the particular dimensions of the site/property plan and the project plan should be noted.**
- **Most ground elevations at the exterior of the building**—at planned parking lots, at the building corners, at all exit doors, at main entrances, and at all sloping ground in the area—need to be shown with the field elevation layouts. Also, **the architects need to relate all site elevations are working with and about sloping sidewalks**, the neighbors' property site elevations too, just in case, the different levels of the two properties are next to each other. In such case, the separated retaining wall to support the higher level ground will be required.
The ground slab and landing elevations must provide ADA access, including door sill details. With this information, the architect needs to plan the budget for removal or addition of soil in specific areas. Civil/Structural engineers or geotechnical consultants **should confirm whether it is necessary to add, replace, and remove existing soil.** Such conditions will also control the type of foundation; such as deep piles, the size of concrete foundations, enclosing retaining walls or other possibilities.
- It is necessary to plan the design decisions regarding accessibility of the water supply, drainage pipes, and electrical supply by the surrounding city, state, or the other properties.

It is wise to let the client know about possible unavoidable budget improvements. To adjust the uplifted cost estimates, some agency clients may plan to control their number of projects scheduled for each year, to capture the cost of a unique project.

Construction Documents

New Residential House-Type 2

Proposed House Model

All rooms have views towards the water bay.

FLOOR PLANS
b. Floor Plans

Residential building planning advocates and determines clients' daily living status and should be impacted considering the surrounding views.

Public buildings:

The following items could be able to adjust the approach to the installation of interior walls during construction. All dimensions throughout the total width and length of the building should be noted. **Since the specific program rooms and especially exit corridors require precise dimensions, other rooms such as storage could be shown with a +/- dimensions.** (This item is noted because often, the built room sizes may vary from a half inch to two to three inches—if not even larger size differences.) When a storage room is noted with +/- proper dimensions, the general construction status will support going forward with required sizes of the main exit planned spaces such as corridors and, rooms such as theaters, classrooms or science classrooms.

• Other series of dimension lines could be partially related to certain significant and major places.

• **Every size of the walls should take into account the thickness of its finish materials.** Otherwise, the exit area widths are reduced by one inch or more, and the building inspectors may object to the relevance of not meeting the exit dimension requirements at corridors, stair-flight width or depths of landings.

• Restroom dimensions must be planned correctly to meet criteria for wheelchair access and turning door openings, and required space in front of sinks or other toilet units for handicapped access.

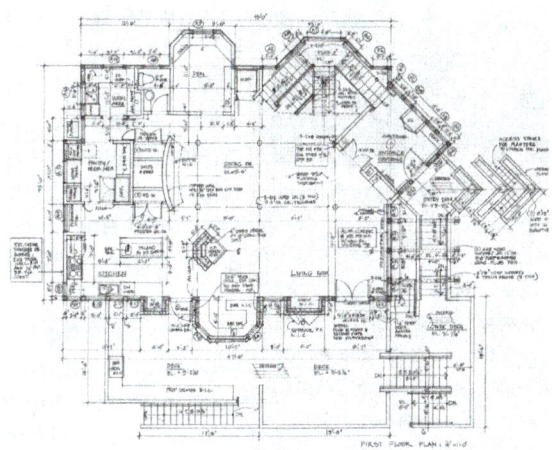

First Floor Plan

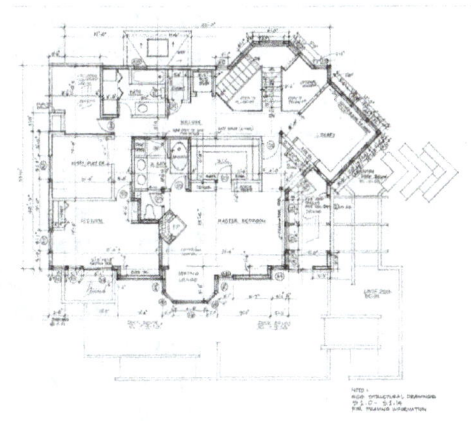

Second Floor Plan

Construction Documents
Consultants' Work Status

See a professional building parapet detail on page no. 60

ROOF PLANS
c. *Roof Plans*

All aspects of the slopes should be reviewed, including at the parapet locations because its heights need to be coordinated with the required minimum heights, such as three feet six inches. When the rooftop slopes are not determined, this specific height requirement is not met as a final approved construction status. Therefore, the required parapet height (typically 3'-6"), should be added in addition to the roof-slope-heights.

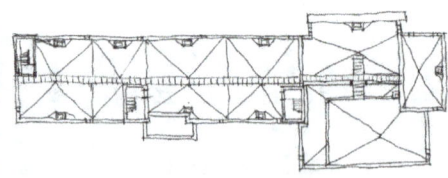

Rooftop plan and parapets- Public High School is shown on page 31

The structural engineer should confirm whether the roof slab structure is adequate to support the load of rooftop appliances. If there are various rooftop devices for serving HVAC, electrical, or water storage tanks, the roof slab structural design details and equipment supports should be checked and confirmed with the structural engineer to satisfy construction, and an overall slab thickness.

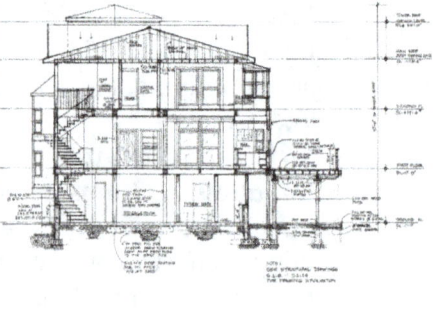

Rooftop equipments at a large size project.

Ideally an architect can make sure that not all units are close to and exposed towards exterior elevations to achieve the design intent.

Waterproofing and other rooftop materials should be finalized with a continuous layer of waterproofing throughout the building height, including all the details of parapets. The waterproofing should continue towards and within exterior wall construction details. The similar materials should also extend downward throughout the window and door header, jamb and sill details and, canopies, balconies or terrace extensions.

House Type 2: A residential building rooftop

BUILDING SECTIONS
d. *Building Sections:*

Major cross sections of the building should be updated at this stage to coordinate appropriately and at least match the comprehensive profiles of the working drawings/ building details. Even though only a few details in the building sections are necessary the profiles need to match the final details shown on other drawings, and the section profile needs to match the final designs to eliminate contractors' questions.

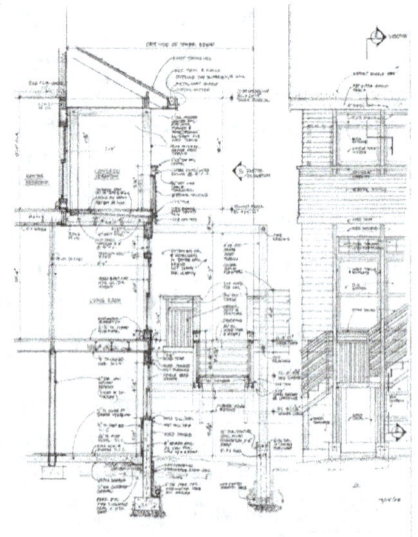

House Type-2: Front entrance and its access to reach the first floor level

Construction Documents

EXTERIOR ELEVATIONS

e. *Exterior Elevations*

In addition to the typical elevations drawings, specific requirements will adhere to proper construction and building design process:

- **All the expansion and control joints** should be located and shown.
- **All windows and doors lintels and supporting units for the exterior finish/ layer material** such as bricks, stone panels, and other reinforcement materials should be already determined and shown with exterior wall details.
- **Window sills, headers, and jambs with some projected canopies** to control sunlight should be designed and indicated on the elevation at best.
- There are possibilities of adjusting/ creating the window surface designs/ direction to control the direct sunlight.
- **At the parapets around the rooftop heights, there are requirements of planning overflow units to manage the water level on the rooftops** as an impact of storms or heavy rains or possible block-ups of any drainpipes. Such items need to be designed as a part of the exterior wall portions and the city or town regulations.

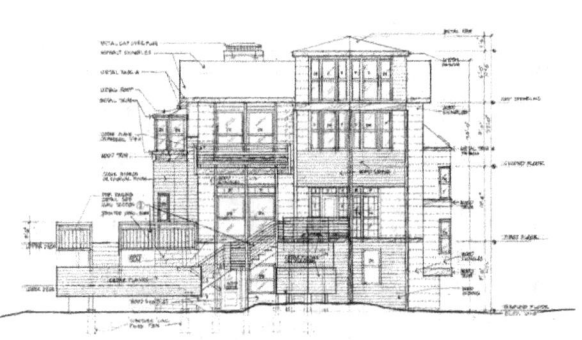

f. *Exterior Wall Sections*

Exterior wall sections should entirely include the building supports, its fire-resistance enclosures, and service elements such as pipes, ducts, electrical cable units, as well as insulation and waterproofing materials. The attached sketches show basic principles that should be formatted. The wall sections should also include the attachments required for the exterior finish surface materials.

House Type 2:
The elevations shown above, are designed to capture every room location and its level to view the bay area.
As profiles of the window header and jamb areas with rectangular canopies projections are shown on pg no. 63

High-rise building: Exterior material dimensions should be considered and propsed to follow and adjust the impact of built structure which sometimes reduces the heights of the entire buildings. Therefore, ideally a strip material near each floor location may not be produced prior to completion of the entire buiding height.

Construction Documents
Consultants' Work Status

The structural slab major-supports were planned to be equal depths in specific areas to maintain the ceiling plans. At vertical wall corners, there are diagonal bracing to strengthen the impact of wind speeds. At some Northeast coast or other areas, the vertical wood studs and upper beams are connected with metal angles and other attachment pieces to strengthen the impacts and resist wind speed and its directions.

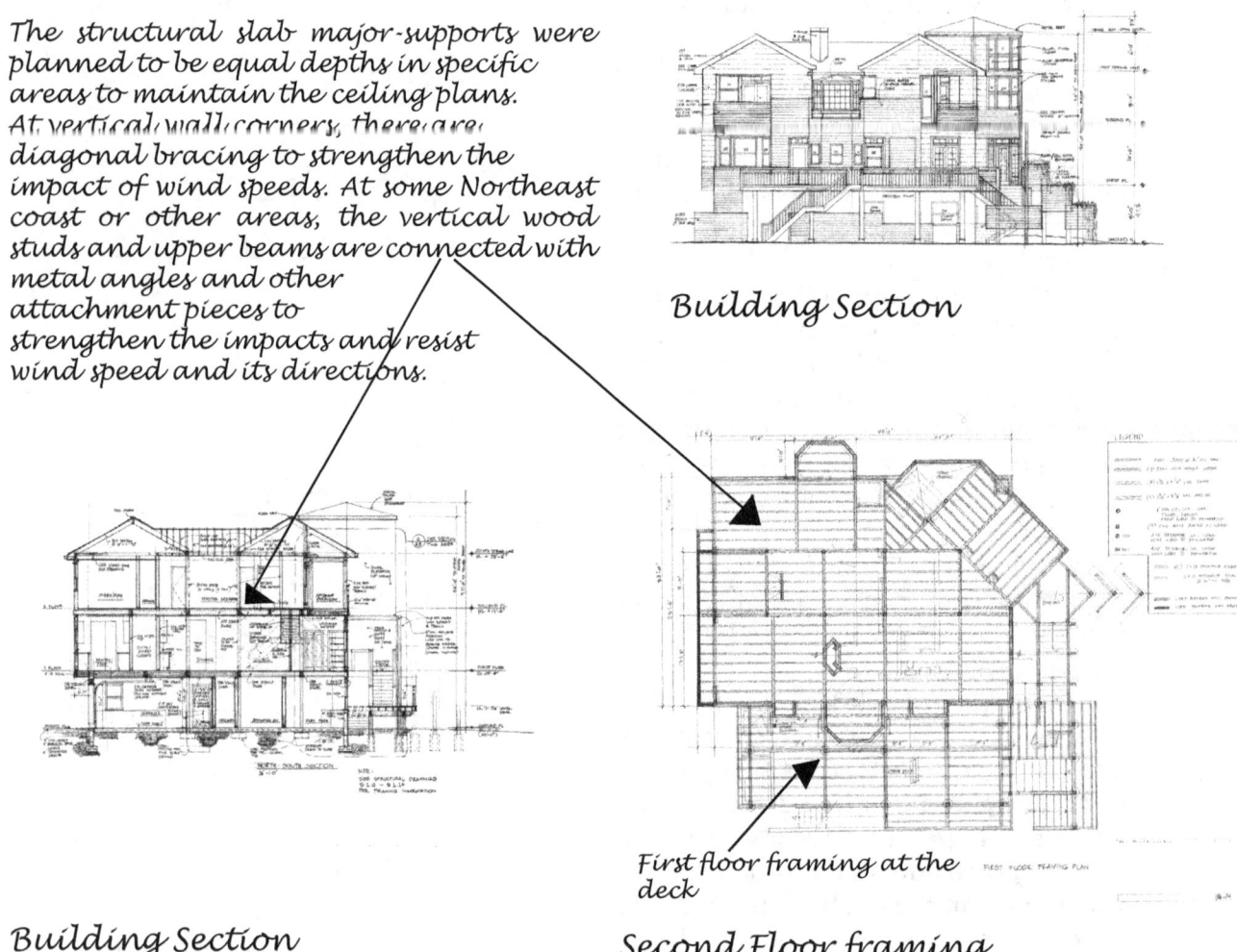

Building Section

First floor framing at the deck

Building Section *Second Floor framing*

CONSULTANT'S WORK STATUS

At each step toward completion of the documents, **it is crucial to gather all requirements for supporting, transferring or maintaining the HVAC, plumbing, and electrical items included in the contract or even future considerations to a reasonable extent.** The architects should meet regularly with engineers because the translations of the ongoing working results may not completely match or assess the proper final versions. In essence, the ultimate accurate products appear after close connections with the consultants' staff rather than proceeding with translations of drawings only, which of course should consistently continue with accuracy.

Otherwise, such questions arise during construction installations and would be processed as change orders by the contractors.

Construction Documents

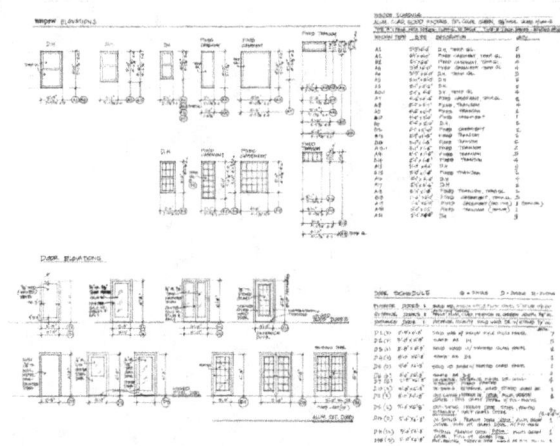

Windows and Doors

SPECIFICATIONS:

Specifications must be finalized entirely during working and construction document sessions. **As a process stated in drawing standards, the specification writing of the items should also be reviewed by the team so that all the specification material qualities and the final result of installation will be correctly specified.** Sometimes the project specification documents need to be different from standard specification documents typically maintained by the firms.

As an experience, **at times one would need to write about restoration and renovation material specification which do not always exist as the standard specifications in the office.** As mentioned above, all details and systems of installation should be determined to write the specification for the entire process of installation of those materials, **also by formatting some expert sub-contractors' recommendations.**

REALISTIC CONSTRUCTION PROCESS VS. STANDARD CATEGORY

The architects need **to assemble the primary intent of the project results by establishing their participation both based on standard classification of the contract work or, the designed project categories** and expected results by the communities as well as the professional success.

Such proficiency will be based on the drawings, documents, specifications and bidding agreements with the contractors. Therefore, the architects could suggest the clients about necessities before and during the construction process to determine the final results and gaining the project status by checking the significant building process.

Bidding Process

Contents

BIDDING PROCESS

BIDDING PROCESS SUGGESTIONS

The bidding process often lasts for six to eight weeks and is usually handled by the client with input from architects, engineers, and other consultants. Because the client often does not know the typical process of material installations, all suggestions and questions that apparently, the contractors send, the architects and consultants need to be ready to provide the answers and drawing improvements as required.

Therefore, the clients and professionals may discuss the building process before, and while the contractors are submitting their bid response during usually six weeks or possibly maximum eight-to ten weeks.

Bidding Process

BIDDING PROCESS

The bidding process, most of the times handled by the client with the architect's, help to provide the set of drawings, specifications, surveys, and some of the code approval aspects and, explanations of the critical project implications.

To ensure that the final design is not compromised, **the architect should insist on using the superior available materials selected without any replacement options.**

Additional efforts could be furnished by the architect to achieve the confirmed material provisions, installation process, and estimates. The professional architect could arrange to deliver the scope of efforts indicating some major or all requirements. **If it is helpful to reach, present, and insist on the most material samples to be shown during the Bid-meetings, its availability and offer discussions regarding the importance of using those materials** without any replacement options. Such process maintains the final result of built buildings and *success of the design excellence.*

During the bidding period, contractors often submit questions regarding construction systems and even time adjustments. **When this approach goes on, the architect needs to explain, provide, and present the answers and revise the drawings and specifications as required to achieve confirmation.** Such conditions should also be reaffirmed during the bid meetings with the contractors. Since the contractors have a limited time to submit their bid documents, the architect could confirm the above questions and answers before, finalizing the selection of the contractor by the clients.

It is vital for the client to start construction on time, in which case the architects should spend some time to recapture all additional clarification details or specifications as required. Then they should create the revisions and inclusions using drawings and tell the client that they are necessary for the bidding process. The architects should be ready to answer all questions as well as make suggestions. **They could always display the mock-ups and material samples they gathered so that contractors know that they cannot change the materials, or expectations, or timeline for building completion.**

BIDDING PROCESS SUGGESTION

A few times, a certain number of contractors are selected to provide the bids. The architects should just review and find sufficient information about a forthcoming couple of possible top selections of the contractors to support and advise the clients.

Also, **as we know, only certain contractors ask for RFI (Requests for Information) answers to process the bidding with a reasonable and practical side of construction.** Whereas, some other contractors who want to receive the selection as a contractor may not proceed to ask such RFIs. As a result, this status of the project turns into extra payments later, for example, *change order methodologies.*

Project Site Supervision

Project Site Supervision

Most of the time, site supervisions by the hired original architects and consultants result as a successful version of built-buildings. The firms should also rely on proper information and successful release of the construction process known by their in-house or hired supervisors.

Regarding a few Agency-projects, which may have been supervised by their staff, will be reviewed by their architects occasionally as requested by the agencies. Such operation may endure a limited version of the design excellence.

Project Site Supervision

Contents:

REVIEW OF DRAWING, SPECIFICATIONS, AND COSTS

SAMPLES AND MOCK-UPS

RELATIONSHIP WITH THE CONTRACTORS

DIGITAL COMPUTER STATUS

SITE ISSUES, RELATIVE ACTIONS, AND FINAL CONSTRUCTION RESULTS

CONSTRUCTION SUPERVISION

Project Site Supervision

PROJECT SITE SUPERVISION

REVIEW OF DRAWING, SPECIFICATIONS, AND COSTS

The architects and the supervisors should read and understand the specifications, drawings, exact dimensions, and prices so that they can provide the correct answers to questions from contractors. **Also before supervising any item, the architect should think about how they would be installed, constructed, and finished.** Unless the architects and consultants determine the realistic process of material installations, the answers to the contractors may not be as appropriately active, as required. Furthermore, often the contractors may not add their supporting installation process but would want to claim a change order on the same subject and materials.

SAMPLES AND MOCK-UPS

This review should be completed before starting the supervision. One more process is, in some renovation items in the specifications—the architect can ask and write about a sample mock-up as many times as needed- for its approvals by them to finalize the installation. **Thereby, the contractor in that project cannot stop preparing and presenting an adequate sample because of such fundamental specification status.**

RELATIONSHIP WITH THE CONTRACTORS

With the knowledge of all documents, the architect should manage, supervise and discuss the details at important construction meetings with the contractors to answer their difficult questions and sometimes, complaints during construction.

But finally, we should always have a good relationship with the subcontractors. Thus, they could do the best sample mock-ups. **The result of all this type of supervision, as well as contractors' work, has been proved in a previously built building that stands and looks like a newly constructed building over the past twenty years.**
Therefore, this is the substance that one could intend to recognize the award-winning projects.

DIGITAL COMPUTER STATUS

Recent perceptions, discussions and presented information regarding specifications, drawings, standard detail drawings, or pictures kept typically only on a computer may be followed to proceed with the project but may not necessarily finish with the final result of adequately detailed building construction by the contractors. Realistically the installers and construction workers need a visual status of details continuously to see at the site locations. **Therefore, the architects should consider a realistic approach to finalizing the original good design and building status, specifically on the paper documents.**

Project Site Supervision

House Type 1 - Most of the time, site supervisions by the hired original architects and consultants result as a successful version of built-buildings. The above project is a result of such theory.

SITE ISSUES, RELATIVE ACTIONS, AND FINAL CONSTRUCTION RESULTS

It is also important to record by writing or sketching the site conditions related to the details shown in the drawings. In the working drawings, imagine the complication of timing to complete the answers to the contractors to achieve this. For medium and large projects, some assistants should work with the site supervisor to finish this process and be ready to continue the successful and timely completion of the project.

CONSTRUCTION SUPERVISION

Based on the project contract with the clients' activities and their business status such as City Agencies, developers, and their cultural venue or historical preservation support, the architects' responsibilities will be controlled to various extents. But after all, the final results of the built buildings and the environment of the project needs to be successful with architects' efforts.

Index

Index

A

ADA Ramps: 33

B

the bidding process, 73, 84, 85
budget estimates, 55, 61
building process, 79-83

C

code approvals, 15
construction document, 76, 77, 80
the construction process, 62, 74, 83
construction supervision, 22, 89
consultants' work status, 82

D

design development, 11, 56, 58, 61, 65
design process, 25, 28-36
doors, 64

E

entrance lobbies, 38
exterior design, 41, 43, 48, 49, 60, 81
exterior elevations, 81

F

feasibility study, 10, 12, 14-16
floor planning, 30, 34, 43, 44, 59, 79

H

hi-rise residential building, 54

I

interior design, 11, 28, 34, 36, 37-39, 43, 44, 61, 66-72
interior designers, 61, 68

L

landscaping, 27-29,
locations, 28, 32-36, 63

Index

M

major documents, 77
material selections, 62

P

painting, 70, 71
planning, 27, 29, 31, 34-37, 44, 58, 59, 45, 50
preliminary design, 25-31
program study and diagrams, 28, 30, 31, 33, 39
project development and schedule, 46, 47

R

residential house and projects, 36, 52-54
renovations, 40
RFPs (Request for Proposal), 10, 20-23
the rooftop drainage system, 30
roof plans, 80

S

schematic design, 10, 24, 26, 32-55
sheets, major document, 76, 77
site conditions, 15, 41, 78
site and property planning, 28-29
site supervision, 11, 86-88
space planning, 59
specifications, 64, 83, 89

W

windows, 63
working models, 43, 50, 51, 53, 59, 61

PPaP

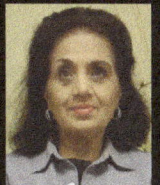

The author, Kalavati Somvanshi–FAIA, RA, AIA, B.Arch. Degree with first class first and design excellence award, G.D.Arch, AAJJA (maiden name: Kala Parab)– graduated in Sir JJ College of Architecture in Bombay (Mumbai), India - and achieved B.Arch and G.D.Arch degrees. Kala worked with two architectural firms until 1965 in India. In a career spanning forty-seven years, Kala has worked in various countries–England, Canada, and the United States- gaining experience in architecture and interior design with a significant escapade in the United States working for forty-three years; of which she spent thirty-four years working in New York City.

Kala is a Registered Architect, FAIA; as has been elected to the College of Fellows of the American Institute of Architects (AIA) and, a life member of the Alumni Association of Sir JJ College of Architecture (AAJJA). Her extensive projects with the prominent firms in the United States are public libraries, museums, planetarium, public high schools, high-rise condominium, City-Hall, site/urban planning & office buildings (all worth $90-$214 million, and variable costs). She also self-practiced many private houses designed and were built using her practice, individually. Working through all phases of architecture practice Kala has innovated some specific suggestions to work with and usable for initially practicing architects.

She worked with the following firms:
Pheroze Kudianawala & Associates, and Gregson, Batley & King Architects, Bombay, India, for three years.
Chamberlin, Powell & Bonn, Architects, London, UK., for one and a half years.
Gaboury, Lussier, Sigurdson, Venables Architects, Manitoba, Canada, for one year.
Setter Leach and Lindstrom, Architects & Engineers, Minneapolis, Minn., for nine years.
Edward Durrell Stone Associates, New York, for six years
Hardy Holzman Pfeiffer Associates, New York, NY., and Los Angeles, CA., entirely for ten years.
Misra & Associates, New York, NY., for fifteen months.
Ennead Architects / Polshek Partnership Architects, LLP, New York, NY., for almost fifteen years.

www.ingramcontent.com/pod-product-compliance
Lightning Source LLC
Chambersburg PA
CBHW081157070526
44583CB00021B/2880